*To Ling – gone but never forgotten.*
*Every time the sky looks magical – like the neons of*
*an orange sunset, or a giant glowing moon – I think of you.*

this book belongs to

. . . . . . . . . . . . . . . . . . . . . . . . . . . . . . . .

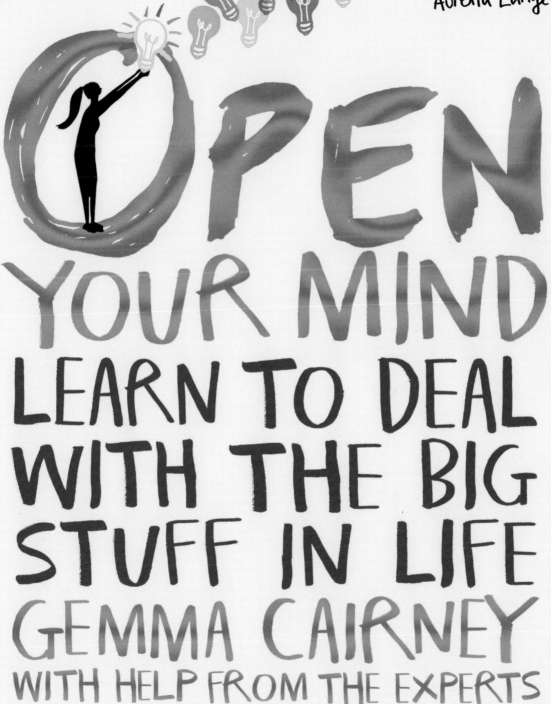

Illustrated by
Aurelia Lange

# OPEN YOUR MIND

## LEARN TO DEAL WITH THE BIG STUFF IN LIFE

### GEMMA CAIRNEY

#### WITH HELP FROM THE EXPERTS

**MACMILLAN**

First published 2017 as part of *Open: A Toolkit for How Magic and Messed Up Life Can Be*
by Macmillan Children's Books

This edition published 2018 by Macmillan Children's Books
an imprint of Pan Macmillan
20 New Wharf Road, London N1 9RR
Associated companies throughout the world
www.panmacmillan.com

ISBN 978-1-5098-7700-3

1 3 5 7 9 8 6 4 2

A CIP catalogue record for this book is available from
the British Library.

Designed by Janene Spencer
Printed and bound in China

# CONTENTS

# WELCOME

Welcome to *Open Your Mind: Learn to Deal With the Big Stuff In Life*.

This book is here to be your guide in times of need. Keep it on your shelf and go to specific chapters during those moments in life that mess with your head, or leaf through and devour it cover to cover. By opening this book you have become part of #TeamOpen, and part of the movement for open hearts and minds. There is no one that this book isn't for.

During years of presenting, and more recently with *The Surgery* on BBC Radio 1, I've encountered a huge variety of people who are dealing with lots of different things in their own ways. My own life hasn't always been easy, and whilst I've dealt with some of the stuff that comes up in this book, I'm not an expert in everything – all I can do is communicate openly about what I've been through and be a friend. I've consulted lots of people who are experts in the issues covered, though – along with a list of people and organizations to speak to if you need more information on anything.

This book covers some tough stuff, but there's nothing you wouldn't find in the storyline of a popular soap opera, and definitely NOTHING you wouldn't find within a four-second Google search. *Open Your Mind* is about real life and everything that comes with it.

This book isn't all about me, it's also about you and all the other incredibly clever, brutally honest, brave and awesomely inspiring voices woven within its pages. This book is yours and I want you to personalize it in any way you see fit; to embellish it and make your own mark on the pages. There are no rules. Douse it in gorgeous gold pen, doodle across it with a blunt pencil or a defiant marker pen, or cover it in magical stickers – and whatever your approach, feel free to respond to however the words make you feel.

Just 🐝 you

# DEAR READER

I write this from Ghana, West Africa, where I am recording a documentary about music for BBC Radio 4.

I have been procrastinating woefully about writing this introduction. Putting off things that you are capable of doing is a type of self-harm. The worry keeps you up at night, oozing around your mind like treacle. But now that I'm in the sun where I'm most happy, in new and uplifting surroundings, my bones feel warm and relaxed, my brain feels more fluid and my beating heart less panicked. I can write this. Self-sabotage is something that comes annoyingly easily to me, but it is also something I've learned to swim with in the seas of life. I know my mind – its ups, its downs, its capabilities – and that helps.

We're all capable in our own ways of learning from hard times, from mistakes and feelings that are difficult to describe but can seem overwhelming. Tuning into behaviours that make you feel down, upset or fearful is a truly powerful thing. It's one of the ways we open our minds. Knowing what makes us us as individuals, accepting it, and deciding to do what makes us feel most happy is the spirit of *Open Your Mind*, the third book in the #TeamOpen family. Be absurd, be berserk, be angst ridden sometimes, surf your own waves, be excited, be bewildered, but don't give in to fear.

I once interviewed the legendary singer Grace Jones, a phenomenal force of a woman; she was utterly brilliant. One of the many marvellous things she said when I asked what scared her was, 'The only thing I fear is fear itself.' It's important to know that our minds are complicated and they need to be exercised just like our limbs.

## 'The only thing I fear is fear itself.'

Sometimes I feel like my body is in knots, like a physical manifestation of exhaustion from being the best I can be, or sadness about failed loves or general life worries. We all need to reset mentally and physically sometimes and we all do it in different ways.

I don't meditate, though I probably should because my mind often fizzes with ideas and fears. Instead, I plunge into cold water, quite literally and metaphorically. I jump into an eighty-year-old tidal pool near my house and splash about like a goofy seal. The way the cold makes my skin tingle and the blue of the ocean fills my vision makes me feel serene. I am immersed in nature, detached from a phone or any technology buzzing at me to buy something, or achieve, or get back to someone on email. It's a mighty flipping powerful way of resetting. (Of course, cold water swimming isn't for everyone and you need to do your research first before starting something new. Don't just jump straight in, but do take the sentiment.) My thing is pool plunging; what's yours? What do you have in your life that you love, that helps you press reset if you're feeling blue? If you don't know the answer, I can only hope that this book will help you find it.

# receiving the book with open arms

It's fair to say that I felt overwhelmed by how many things I touched on in trying to create #TeamOpen and cans of worms were opened in my own personal life. I slumped a little. It's been a heart-wrenching journey, but one I'm truly grateful for. The response I've had since the original hardback *Open, A Toolkit For How Magic and Messed Up Life Can Be* was published has been incredible. I feel inspired and humbled by how awesome people have been in receiving the book with open arms. Knowing that #TeamOpen is out there and that some part of *Open* has made someone giggle, or helped someone to feel less lonely is a thing I can't put into words except for WOW.

Gemma

# YOUR MIND

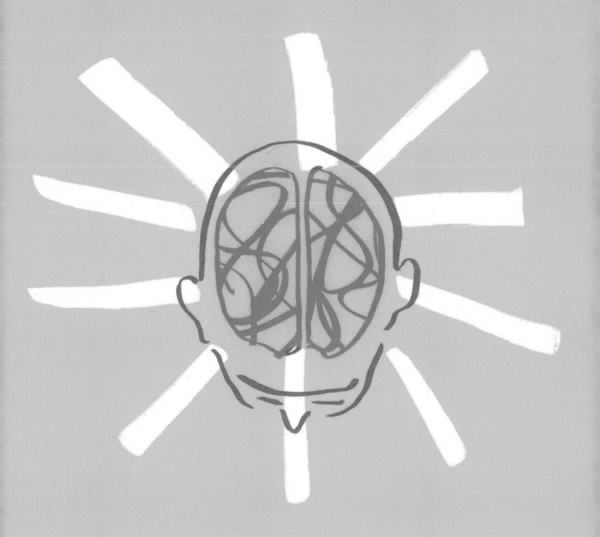

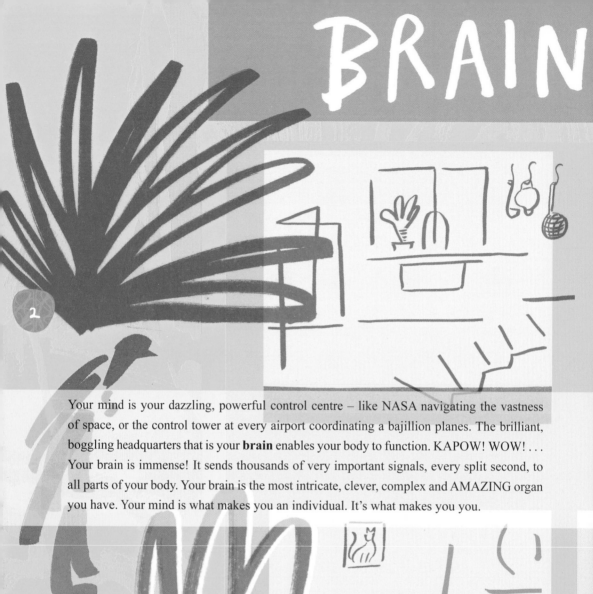

Your mind is your dazzling, powerful control centre – like NASA navigating the vastness of space, or the control tower at every airport coordinating a bajillion planes. The brilliant, boggling headquarters that is your **brain** enables your body to function. KAPOW! WOW! . . . Your brain is immense! It sends thousands of very important signals, every split second, to all parts of your body. Your brain is the most intricate, clever, complex and AMAZING organ you have. Your mind is what makes you an individual. It's what makes you you.

# HOUSE

While you're growing – from birth to adult-hood – your brain is developing impressively fast. You learn to crawl, to speak, to read and write, to ride a bike . . . to drive, to cook, to perhaps even speak another language. Your brain is exotic, inquisitive and capable of all sorts. You are endlessly grabbing at the multiple learning opportunities the world around you has to offer with the help of your brain. Stop and give your incredible mind some credit for a second.

You may feel like a loser sometimes – but you were once merely a tiny cell . . . and now look at you! Snap, crackle, POP! – your brain is whirring. If you're lucky, and you protect it, your brain will serve you well. Combined with positive experiences, education, nurturing and the right people around you, your brain will help you make important life decisions, alert you to danger and keep you on the right path.

But sometimes, through no fault of your own, your brain can let you down.

This section of the book will walk you through some important truths about the way our minds work. We'll explore some of the darker corners, and give you the knowledge and the tools to cope when things go wrong. Please read on, especially if you are experiencing issues with your mental health or feeling at a loss in trying to help out a family member or friend.

RANDOM
BRAIN-FACT KLAXON . . .
THE REASON YOU CAN'T TICKLE
YOURSELF IS BECAUSE YOUR BRAIN
CAN INSTANTLY DISTINGUISH BETWEEN
UNEXPECTED EXTERNAL TOUCH AND YOUR OWN.
YOUR BRAIN IS WELL CLEVER!

FYI — I love
tickling people.

4

66 If we think about ourselves as brains . . . the brain is a lot about thinking, but the brain is also a lot about feeling. In fact, in Western society we have an obsession sometimes with the brain as a thinking thing, you know, in terms of exams, in terms of being smart, in terms of wordiness and so on — and so on — but actually there's as much of the brain dedicated to feeling as there is to thinking. 99

**Dan Glaser, neuroscientist**

Understanding your brain and your mind ain't half TOUGH sometimes.

## EVERYDAY ANXIETY ABOUT LIFE

# DO YOU EVER FEEL LIKE YOUR HEAD IS IN A CLAMP?

Do you sometimes feel so overwhelmed by life that your mind feels numb and dumb? Are you weary from just thinking so much? Do you feel rinsed out from asking yourself so many questions?

Am I doing the right thing? Do I have the right feeling? What do I eat? Who do I love? Am I working hard enough at my studies, my job, at being a good friend or partner or family member?

I grant you this moment to scream. Yes, SCREAM. OK, don't alarm your neighbours into thinking you are being attacked. But just let it out, that vital and necessary SCREAM . . . Do it into a pillow, or on a rollercoaster, during an orgasm, playing sport or underwater at your local swimming pool. If you feel like life is getting truly annoying, it's OK to scream responsibly.

# LIFE ISN'T ALWAYS
## easy

'Well, it's weird, isn't it?' said my friend Laurence recently, whilst sat around a dinner table philosophizing and trying to work out the meaning of life. 'Being heaps of bones encased in flesh and filled with feelings.'

We were pondering political doom and whether we were making the right life choices. Let's face it: being human is weird. It's weird to sometimes panic that life is too short – and then at other times wish time away. It's weird to want everything to be perfect, but not know what perfect is. We are big, walking, talking contradictions really. Let's just accept that and try to find a middle ground, some calm and acceptance . . .

**It is NOT good for your mind to . . .**

- **bitch about others**

- **obsessively check in with your phone, rather than your real life**

- **worry about something out of your physical control**

- **judge others**

- **do things that you fundamentally don't agree with – just to please others.**

# DEMONS

**Demons.** Those nagging obstacles to your peace of mind. They are snarling, weaselly, toad-like things, and they are annoying to say the least. They wield defiant little pickaxes, and their mission is to get right into your noggin,* making you anxious, stressed and upset.

*__Noggin__: a word my cherub of a friend Georgia uses to describe our heads. I love it because it makes our heads seem almost funny.

These demons don't half piss me off, and when I imagine what mine might look like I imagine jumping, blobby, chewed-up bubble-gum balls with poppy-out eyes and big, licking tongues. We each have our own particular demon(s), made up of many things. If we were labelling their ingredients – what they're made up of – they'd contain half a tablespoon of nature (things we are born with – our DNA and genetic make-up), a dash of nurture (how we are brought up, environmental influences), a sprinkling of regret, perhaps the odd trauma and a dollop of fear thrown in for good measure.

Depending on how big and defiant they are, demons are pretty good at getting in the way of life, and they can make us feel out of control. Some people's demons manifest as a sense of isolation; others come as startling anxiety or a panic attack. Some appear as a dark cloud of depression, or as an addiction that grips. Demons are bespoke.

It's good to equip ourselves by KNOWING OUR DEMONS and how they make us feel. Stare them in the face and figure out exactly what we're scared of . . . and – most importantly – WHY we're scared of whatever it might be.

To put it simply: if we can identify the roots of our problems, they aren't as likely to bubble up to boiling point inside us.

Opening up about your demons – big and small – is the first step to getting on better with those pesky toads. There is nothing to be ashamed of: you are a human being, you are dealing with a lot and it's time to offload.

What do your demons look like? Draw them below.

# FYI . . .

**. . . SINCE CAVE TIMES**, we have been tuned in to risk and danger. 'Fight or flight', as the survival response is known, was once upon a time about hunting for food and not getting eaten – these days, our anxiety is about exams, money and terrorism. Some of us soak it up more than others. For some, **fear and anxiety** are all too familiar, and **calmness and happiness** seem harder to find. If this is you – THIS DOESN'T MEAN your life is crap. If this applies to someone you know – and that someone finds reaching a calm mental state a struggle – it doesn't make them less of a person . . . it's just the way their brain is wired.

# THE BIG DEMON DETONATORS

**The main factors that feed your demons** and that can mess with your mental health are:

# STRESS

# TRAUMA

# ANXIETY

They can be caused by external factors such as:

- **Other human beings inflicting pain on to or adding pressure to our lives.**
- **Media/advertising.**
- **Pressure and expectation to achieve/look/behave a certain way.**
- **Traumatic experiences.**

These factors are sometimes out of our control. When we are feeling unhappy, it can be difficult to define why, or to put a finger on exactly where our unhappiness is coming from. These things can swirl together, turning our heads into a pot of steaming mashed potato. Sometimes it is really hard to know what's going on.

I am no stranger to the mashed potato swirl myself. I wear my heart right out and fleshy on my sleeve. I think deeply. I cry deeply. I feel truly, madly, deeply on occasion. Sometimes, this dramatic streak in my nature has threatened to overwhelm me. The plus side of having a mind like mine is it means I have an extraordinary imagination – sometimes my head feels like it contains fireworks.

These days, as a grown woman, I mostly feel genuinely humbled by the brilliance of life and the beautiful things about it – like friendships, conversations and the limitlessness of creativity – all of which keep me warm, happy and feeling safe. But that is now. My lowest point was some time ago – in my early twenties, during a period of big confusion, growing pains, abusive relationships and raw grief. Like many others, I was prescribed antidepressants. Personally, medication wasn't for me. I knew that I needed to deal with my muddled mass of feelings another way.

Led by instinct, I spent time scouring 'alternative therapy' options online and came across a course of 'tapping therapy', which I personally found amazing. Alternative therapies don't have to cost a lot of money. At that time, I was broke, so I searched HIGH AND LOW to find someone who would help for no more per treatment than it would cost me to go to the cinema. Before you embark on ANY type of therapy, you do need to make sure that you are going to someone both recommended and qualified. So do your research, especially before you embark on alternative therapies. They're not for everyone, but in my opinion – when it comes to matters of the mind – they can be worth investigating and fun to explore.

'I have never met anyone who wanted to feel better so much,' said the angelic alternative therapy lady, who yanked me out of my hole of misery. And all by tapping me whilst I cried. It worked for me.

Please note: Medication is vital for many who suffer from depression and other mental-health-related conditions. It helps them function, and it can save lives. If you have been prescribed antidepressants, please talk to your doctor if you feel you don't need them, and certainly before you stop taking them.

To make better sense of the demon detonators, it helps to know exactly what they are and how they present themselves.

*Note: Dr Caroline Taylor, a chartered clinical psychologist, has provided the science bits!*

## WHAT IS STRESS?

### THE SCIENCE BIT:

14

Stress is the experience of being overwhelmed with what we need to do, or think we need to do. Stress happens when we think we don't have the skills, or time, to achieve these things. Unfortunately, thinking that we are unable to do something, and worrying or feeling scared about our perceived inability, makes us more stressed, and so more overwhelmed.

## My non-scientific explanation:

Stress is a bit like being in a pressure cooker (I imagine, anyway – as, strangely, I've never been in a pressure cooker!). Your palms might sweat, or you might wake up in a worry fog that you can't shift. When I'm stressed, I can feel adrenalized, a bit helpless, sometimes downbeat, and then guilty about feeling those things – sometimes all at the same time.

## WHAT IS ANXIETY?

**THE SCIENCE BIT:**

Anxiety is the bodily and emotional response to danger or threat. It gives us important information about the situation we are currently in. Anxiety arrives when a hormone called adrenaline is released into our bodies in the face of danger. It often feels very uncomfortable, and makes us want to get away from the emotion and the danger. In this sense, anxiety is our friend — it keeps us safe. If we 'suffer' from anxiety, it is likely that we believe that something will harm us or is a danger to us. Our brain is fine-tuned to stay alert for danger at any given moment, to keep us alive and well. But this means our brain is always searching for threats — and when it finds one it releases adrenaline, even if there is no real danger to our lives. For example, we might get anxious when we revise — not because learning is life-threatening, but because we fear not passing the exam, and the impact that would have on our future.

# My non-scientific explanation:

Hurricane-like swirls of anxiety inside us make it feel really difficult to get on with things that we might otherwise find 'easy' – like interacting with people, working or getting from one place to another. These feelings can be described as panic attacks, and they can feel frightening . . . but they do pass.

## THE SCIENCE BIT:

Trauma means harm or damage, whether it be physical, psychological, emotional — or all three at the same time. So, for example, someone could be physically injured in a road traffic accident, and be psychologically damaged by the experience — especially if they thought they (or someone they were with) were going to die (or did die). Physical trauma is generally easier to treat than emotional or psychological trauma, mainly because the effects of the physical trauma are easier to understand and see.

16

## My non-scientific explanation:

Like a savings bank made up of fear and sadness in your head, trauma can result in phobia, discomfort and pain stored up in our brains. It can be triggered by even the tiniest thing, by our brain's association with whatever ingredients are at the root of our trauma. It is important to identify what these ingredients and triggers are and to recognize what is happening to you. Only then can you give yourself the care you need.

PLEASE REMEMBER: If you can identify with any of this stuff, you are definitely not mad or bad. No one is completely OK all the time. Life affects us in different ways, and our mental health is easily challenged. If and when it is challenged severely, it can be deeply painful and confusing and, most importantly, it can affect your behaviour, your perspective and your ability to cope.

No one's mind reacts to the world in exactly the same way, but if you've experienced any of these demon detonators then you might find that the balance between bleakness and brightness in your brain feels a bit wonky. If that is the case for you or someone you know, then read on. The next section covers the different ways your brain can react to your demons.

# SOCIAL ANXIETY DISORDER

It's OK to be you, however you are. It's OK to be shy. But social anxiety is more than shyness. If you are consistently feeling shy or awkward or anxious to an overwhelming degree and it is preventing you from identifying the joy to be found in life, then you may be suffering from something more serious than everyday anxiety.

**I hear it from many different types of people. About how the world goes echoey, how it feels like it might burst, how you try to speak but the words won't come out right, because you are unexpectedly afraid of all that is around you. That body-tightening moment of despair at just how crippling social anxiety can be. But when does it become a disorder?**

## Signs of social anxiety disorder

Anxiety from time to time – like when you meet someone new, or you fancy someone, or you have been looking forward to an event for zonks, forever and ever, and then it arrives and you are a ball of anxiety – is part of life. But if it's reaching a stage where it stops you from having fun it's time to work on it.

## What to look out for . . .

If you find that you are often tearful – which is seemingly unconnected to any significant or tangible event – or have consistent difficulty in controlling your emotions, or fear going to school or college or taking part in related activities, then these could be signs of social anxiety disorder.

It is important that you can talk to someone openly and honestly about how you feel.

One thing that's good to know is that it's pretty common. Social anxiety disorder is estimated to affect between **ten to fifteen per cent** of people in their lifetime.* Like most of the curves and bends of our minds, the root cause of social anxiety disorder is not always easy to pinpoint in individuals. It could be linked to any 'shake up' of one's life, like a particular event, but it also may not appear to have any link – it is just a gradual accumulation of anxiety.

*Stats from Anxiety Care UK

## Do you find yourself excessively worrying about:

*How you come across?*

*What people think of you?*

*The first impression you give?*

*Upsetting people?*

*Something you previously said or did?*

18

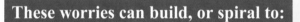

## These worries can build, or spiral to:

- a dread of meeting strangers
- anxiety about or great difficulty in talking to or starting a conversation amongst friends or peers
- anxiety about talking to people in authority, such as teachers or family members
- anxiety about or difficulty with romantic relationships
- studying at school or college, or work
- lack of self-esteem
- drug or alcohol misuse specifically to reduce anxiety

If you're nodding at some of these, then it's time to deal with it. If you haven't told anyone you feel like this, it's time to let those who care about you help and guide you through this time in your life. The strongest mental grip can become looser once you've told people the truth about how hard you find things. Also, talk to yourself. I know this sounds weird, but naming your feelings to yourself out loud really shrinks the power they have over you. Write them down too if you want – to keep in touch with how you feel.

A place
to write down
your feelings

**If someone you know has social anxiety disorder, remember:**

In extreme cases social anxiety disorder can have a disruptive or disabling impact on a person's life. It can severely affect their confidence and self-esteem, interfere with their relationships and impair their performance at work or school. Be patient and tell the person you know they find certain things hard and that's OK.

## Panic attacks and social anxiety disorder

The fear of a social situation or just thinking about things that you are anxious about can sometimes build up to a panic attack, where you experience an overwhelming sense of anxiety and dread. Panic attacks affect different people in different ways, but often cause physical symptoms such as feeling sick, sweating, trembling and heart palpitations. RUBBISH, right? RIGHT, but though alarming, KNOW THIS . . .

- Panic attacks are **NOT** life-threatening.
- The symptoms often **pass quickly**.
- **Help** is all around you – lots of people know how rubbish panic attacks can be and will be happy to help. Whether that's **putting a hand on your shoulder** or leaving you alone for some time to **breathe** or getting you some **water** and being **by your side** . . . Whatever is best for you.
- The most important thing is that you express how you feel and tell people around you what you need from them.

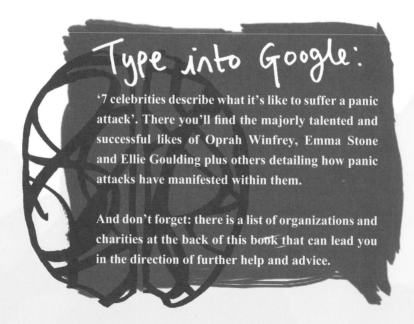

Type into Google:

'7 celebrities describe what it's like to suffer a panic attack'. There you'll find the majorly talented and successful likes of Oprah Winfrey, Emma Stone and Ellie Goulding plus others detailing how panic attacks have manifested within them.

And don't forget: there is a list of organizations and charities at the back of this book that can lead you in the direction of further help and advice.

# DEPRESSION

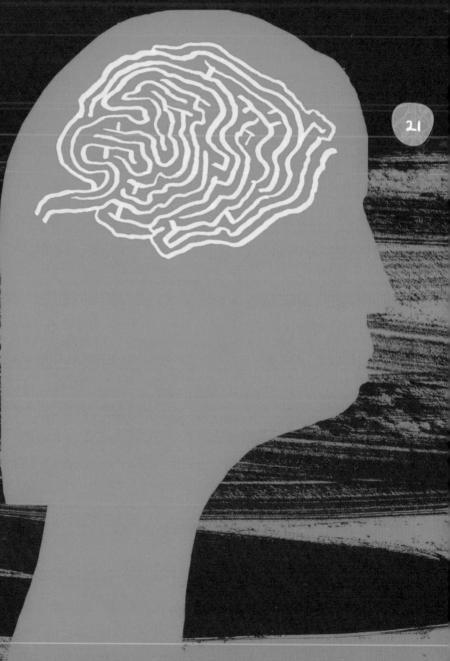

21

When I was at my lowest ebb, I worried that I was a burden to my friends and family. I feared that if I voiced the pain that I was feeling that they would grow tired of me, or that I would, in turn, bring them down too. Of course I was wrong — people want to help, they want to be there, and if you give them the chance they might just surprise you. At the time, I didn't believe this possible. I shrank into myself, and by doing so I gave the power over to my anxiety and OCD, isolating myself further and retreating under the duvet in an attempt to drown out my spiralling thoughts with only Kirsty Young and Desert Island Discs for company. Every morning I would wake, exhausted, after only a couple of hours' sleep, and wish with my whole heart that somebody was there to hold my hand and say, 'Me too.' That was the catalyst for starting #itaffectsme, to let anyone who is suffering with ill mental health know that they are not alone, that there is an army of us fighting, and that, with talking and help, they can get through it, ten seconds at a time.

**Laura Darrall: mental health activist/writer/
actor/kicker of stigma's butt. Founder of
the #itaffectsme viral mental health campaign**

Mental illness has no prejudices about who it affects,
so we should have no prejudices about it.

I asked SANE UK – an awesome, proactive leading mental health charity – to help me break down and define DEPRESSION.

## WHAT IS DEPRESSION?

Depression is different from feeling low and unhappy. It can be triggered by difficult life events, such as bereavement, loss of job or financial worries. But it can also occur when there is no obvious reason due to a chemical imbalance in your brain.

It can vary from person to person, but typically if someone is experiencing low mood, and difficulty sleeping or eating over a period longer than two weeks, then they should consider seeing their GP.

## HOW CAN WE IDENTIFY IT?

It is important to remember that unless you are a mental-health specialist, you are not qualified to make a diagnosis.

But if you do have concerns for someone who is showing these kinds of symptoms it is a good idea to try to gently encourage them to seek professional help through their GP or other qualified specialist.

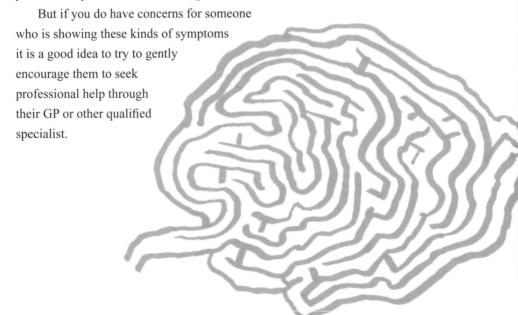

# What does SANE UK do
# to help those who are depressed?

**SANE** provides emotional support and information to anyone affected by mental-health problems like depression, including families, friends and carers.

**SANEline** is a telephone helpline, which is open every evening, every day of the year. There is also a Textcare service that provides supportive text messages at times of need, and an online Support Forum where people can share their experiences and give and receive moral support.

For more information about the services **SANE UK** provides, please visit **www.sane.org.uk**

24

# EATING DISORDERS

FOOD. How do you feel about it?

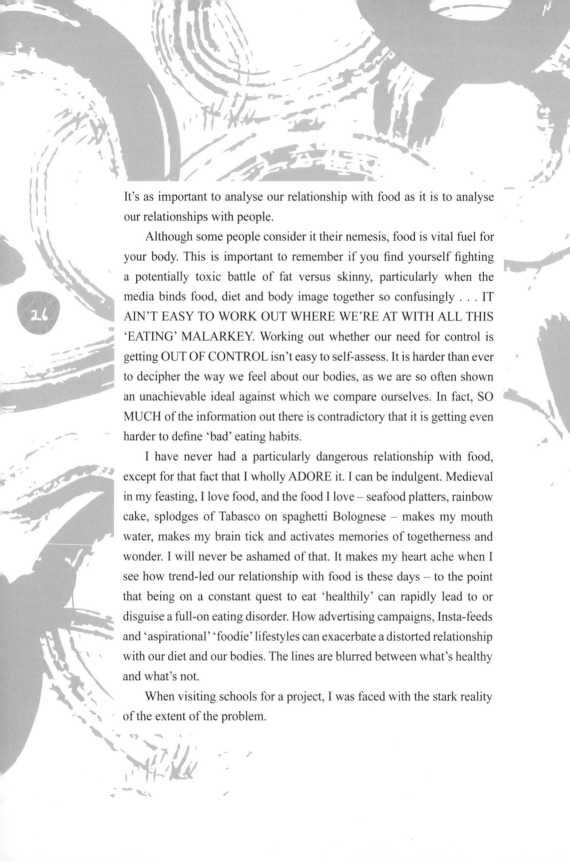

It's as important to analyse our relationship with food as it is to analyse our relationships with people.

Although some people consider it their nemesis, food is vital fuel for your body. This is important to remember if you find yourself fighting a potentially toxic battle of fat versus skinny, particularly when the media binds food, diet and body image together so confusingly . . . IT AIN'T EASY TO WORK OUT WHERE WE'RE AT WITH ALL THIS 'EATING' MALARKEY. Working out whether our need for control is getting OUT OF CONTROL isn't easy to self-assess. It is harder than ever to decipher the way we feel about our bodies, as we are so often shown an unachievable ideal against which we compare ourselves. In fact, SO MUCH of the information out there is contradictory that it is getting even harder to define 'bad' eating habits.

I have never had a particularly dangerous relationship with food, except for that fact that I wholly ADORE it. I can be indulgent. Medieval in my feasting, I love food, and the food I love – seafood platters, rainbow cake, splodges of Tabasco on spaghetti Bolognese – makes my mouth water, makes my brain tick and activates memories of togetherness and wonder. I will never be ashamed of that. It makes my heart ache when I see how trend-led our relationship with food is these days – to the point that being on a constant quest to eat 'healthily' can rapidly lead to or disguise a full-on eating disorder. How advertising campaigns, Insta-feeds and 'aspirational' 'foodie' lifestyles can exacerbate a distorted relationship with our diet and our bodies. The lines are blurred between what's healthy and what's not.

When visiting schools for a project, I was faced with the stark reality of the extent of the problem.

'I only have a miso soup every day for lunch,' said one sixteen-year-old girl, as though she thought it was completely normal.

'But why only that?' I asked.

'Because, I don't want to be fat,' she replied — again in the most chilling, matter-of-fact manner.

It felt like it was only once she voiced this truth that she realized how extreme it sounded. In effect she was starving herself, but most of her peers accepted it as completely normal for her to be monitoring her eating in such a way – the fear of getting fat was far greater than the fear of malnutrition, and a far more relatable idea. I was alarmed. On further investigation, I discovered that she and a friend could sit on Tumblr for up to six hours at a time typing in the word 'skinny' – hours of brainwashing and damaging imagery at their fingertips.

I feel like we need to be having honest conversations when it comes to our relationship with food, and we should listen to ourselves if it's starting to spiral into something dangerous. If it is, it's time to get some help.

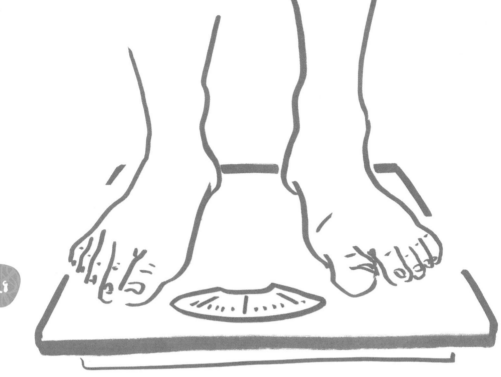

Concerned, I asked Susie Orbach, author of *Fat is a Feminist Issue*, *On Eating*, *Bodies* and *In Therapy* if she had noticed a change in women's attitudes towards their bodies over the years.

 I think the situation is so much worse," she said. "Every inch of our body, every aspect of our bodies has been commercialized, either by the beauty companies, the cosmetic surgery companies, the fashion houses, the food companies, the diet companies. So . . . the situation's much worse, much more unstable . . . The situation with our bodies is pretty serious. We're sort of supposed to have our body as our product rather than the place we live, and that's a really damaging concept.

The world of eating disorders is a complex **mess**. It's dizzying – it's panic-making. It is very trendy to seem in control of your diet. There are so many 'beautiful' people spearheading a bizarre and very money-driven revolution, all in the name of reclaiming our 'health' and 'loving' our bodies. Not all diets or eating plans are suspect, or dangerous, but many are encouraging obsessive behaviour around food. This can lead to eating disorders and send us spiralling out of control. Nutritionist Leo Pemberton says:

> I think one of the dangerous things . . . is that if you follow certain bloggers or Instagram stars, they will all have a slightly different ethos. So if you follow one person and they say, 'I think you should cut out meat, dairy and gluten,' then you also follow someone else and they say, 'You should cut out grains,' then that's where you start to cut out many more groups than those people themselves are cutting . . . If you're cutting out vitamins and minerals and things like calcium or protein from your diet — especially if you're still growing or you're very active — that's when it becomes dangerous and you can run into deficiencies and potentially an eating disorder, which you by no means set out for in the first place.

We all feel like that sometimes. But if it's lodged its way into your mind too firmly, it might be a problem you shouldn't be tackling alone. Eating disorders are very complex and sometimes aren't connected to our relationship with food at all, but perhaps to 'control' or 'self-harm', and sometimes it's a heady mix of all these and more. If you know deep down that things are spiralling, but don't know how to talk about it, a letter is always a good way of reaching out about your feelings and worries.

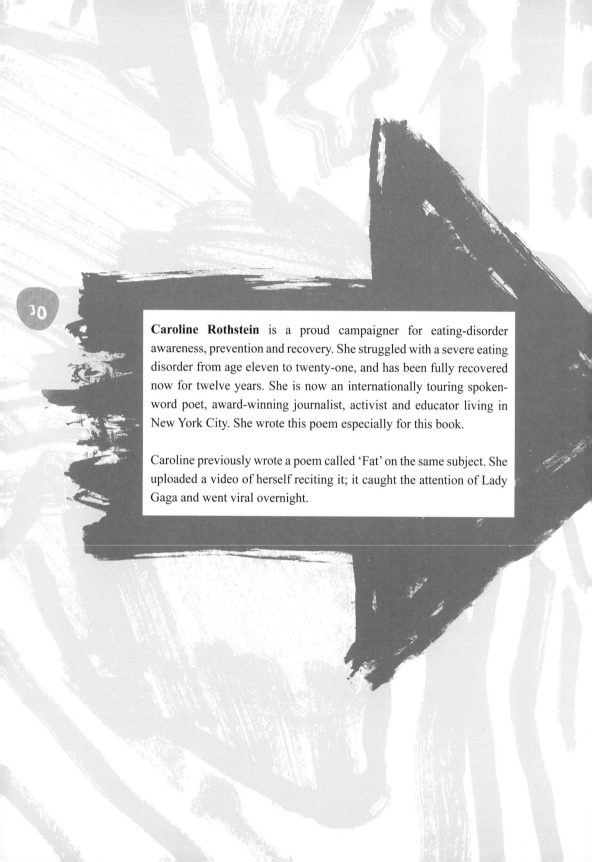

**Caroline Rothstein** is a proud campaigner for eating-disorder awareness, prevention and recovery. She struggled with a severe eating disorder from age eleven to twenty-one, and has been fully recovered now for twelve years. She is now an internationally touring spoken-word poet, award-winning journalist, activist and educator living in New York City. She wrote this poem especially for this book.

Caroline previously wrote a poem called 'Fat' on the same subject. She uploaded a video of herself reciting it; it caught the attention of Lady Gaga and went viral overnight.

# FREE

### by Caroline Rothstein

The time I told my eating disorder it could no longer live rent-free inside of me (the way it etched horror films into the lining of my oesophagus, the way it sacrificed my sanity on the altar of my throat, the way it tummy-tucked trauma into the residue of my fingernails and pierced grief on to the outskirts of my uvula, dangling with ache),

was a good day. It was a Thursday. November 18. Warm enough to forget I had ever seen the sun. Cold enough to forget my deepest secret – that I was enough. Loneliness seemed so sacred, what with the gapping crevices of shame that had atrophied my soul. Though this isn't about the ulcer, or the popped eye blood vessel, or the straight Cs, or

31

the red Solo plastic cups I filled with vomit like other people filled with beer at parties on weekends. This isn't about the suicidal thoughts, or the way I cut my wrist, and my thigh, and my forearm, and prayed that every day I might end up in the hospital so that someone might, in fact, see the pain that was eating me alive now breathing on my skin.

That is the obvious part, really. That is the textbook. That is the shit they make you read in health class when they tell you you're a statistic and make the bullies go home. That's the multi-billion-dollar diet industry that pleads for you to hate yourself so you'll forget the deepest secret – because it isn't just mine – see that's the stuff they'll tell you so that

it too can live rent-free underneath, inside, behind your skin. The time I told my eating disorder to find another home, I didn't want to die any more. I watched my dead brother float around my bedroom and tell me I had a body so wasn't it worth treating it like a temple? Wasn't it worth worshipping everything that lived within? He was there in the

room, my dead brother. And so was awe. And more than anything I saw my soul etched into the lining of my body, sacrificing my hysteria on the altar of my fear, the way it unhinged trauma from the residue of my fingernails and pierced faith into the outskirts of my uvula, dangling with trust. It was a good day when the all-knowing voice within

my stomach opened up into the depths of possibility. When I decided I was enough, and that my body was a triumph. And that resilience was the only prayer I'd ever need to sing. It was a good day when my heart wept for itself. When my brain reconnected with my soul. When the rent went up and recovery moved in and I finally had a tenant-free home.

# OBSESSIVE-COMPULSIVE DISORDER

For a long time, OCD was a condition that was treated almost as a joke – you know, about those who clean obsessively, or are 'neat freaks': 'Oh, they've just got a bit of OCD.' But, make no mistake, OCD is complex and debilitating for those who have it. When you go beneath the surface and see how intensely OCD can affect its sufferers, and how common it is, you know it's a condition not to be taken lightly.

There are two main components to OCD, the obsessions and compulsions, but what combines the two is an intense feeling of anxiety.

In general, OCD sufferers experience obsessions that take the form of persistent and uncontrollable thoughts, images, impulses, worries, fears or doubts. They are often intrusive, unwanted, disturbing and significantly interfere with the ability to function on a day-to-day basis as they are incredibly difficult to ignore.

Compulsions are repetitive physical behaviours and actions or mental thought rituals that are performed over and over again in an attempt to relieve the anxiety caused by the obsessional thoughts. Avoidance of places or situations to prevent triggering these obsessive thoughts is also considered to be a compulsion. But, unfortunately, any relief that the compulsive behaviours provide is only temporary and short lived, and often reinforces the original obsession, creating a gradual worsening cycle of obsessions and compulsive behaviours.

Whilst the public perception of OCD is someone carrying out cleaning or checking compulsive ritualistic behaviours, the reality is that for many people obsessions and compulsions will be internal with no physical manifestation, an example is someone may be overly concerned with fears about sexuality or their relationship and will engage in lots of reassurance and checking, either with themselves or with loved ones.

It is fair to say that to some degree OCD-type symptoms are probably experienced at one time or another by most people. However, the key difference that segregates little quirks, often referred to by people as being 'a bit OCD' from the actual disorder is when the distressing and unwanted experience of obsessions and compulsions impacts to a significant level upon a person's everyday functioning — this represents a principal component in the clinical diagnosis of obsessive—compulsive disorder.

66 By my early twenties, I'd already spent half a decade trying to figure out the meaning of my relentless, graphic sexual thoughts. Maybe I was a self-loathing, homophobic lesbian who just couldn't accept who she was? Then one night, when I was high on antidepressants and Jägermeister, I saw two girls kissing at a house party. It was my light-bulb moment. These girls seemed so free and in love — a million light-years away. With my self-harm and my 24/7 flesh-crawling anxiety and my constant frightening mental images, I was on another planet. I sensed for the first time that I was mental, and googled the words 'intrusive thoughts', and my life changed forever. 99

**Rose Bretécher, former sufferer of pure OCD , a type that includes obsessive, intrusive sexual thoughts. Rose is also the author of *Pure: A Memoir*, which recounts her experiences with and overcoming of OCD.**

# OCD: THE STATISTICS

- Around the world there are literally millions of people affected by OCD, and it is considered to be the fourth most common mental illness in many Western countries, and will affect men, women and children regardless of their race, religion, nationality or socio-economic group.

- Here in the United Kingdom, current estimates suggest that 1.2 per cent of the population will have OCD, which equates to twelve out of every 1,000 people, and based on the current estimates for the UK population, these statistics mean that, potentially, approximately 758,000 people are living with OCD at any one time.

- However, it is worth noting that a disproportionately high number, fifty per cent, of all these cases will fall into the severe category, with less than only a quarter being classed as mild cases. Which is why some estimates suggest that maybe two to three per cent of all those visiting their GP will be doing so because of OCD.

**If any of this sounds familiar and you think that you're showing symptoms of OCD, you don't have to suffer in silence – there is treatment available. Go and see your GP and tell someone you trust about how you're feeling.**

# ADDICTION

When we think of addiction, we often think of alcohol, drugs or cigarettes, but actually an addiction is anything that you can't stop doing or stop thinking about – when you feel like you don't have control over its role in your life. Addiction can have a very serious effect on your mind, your body, your relationships and everything you do. People with more serious addictions often need professional intervention to help them break their damaging habits, and some addictions can even be life-threatening.

It is heartbreaking to watch someone lambast themselves for their addiction, while corroding their body, personality and relationships. And it shouldn't be underestimated how tightly an addiction can grip, and how hard it can be to escape it.

It is possible to be addicted to:

cigarettes    sex
illegal drugs caffeine
Social media exercise
prescribed drugs alcohol
sugar    our phones    porn

# COULD YOU BE ADDICTED?

If you are worried, try taking the test below.

Think about the thing you enjoy the most out of the list of possible addictions on the previous page and write it here:

**Do you . . . (circle your answer)**

| | |
|---|---|
| Crave it? | YES / NO |
| Do you feel relieved once you've used it or consumed it? | YES / NO |
| Do you feel irritable or angry if you are denied it, or try to withdraw from it? | YES / NO |
| Do you feel that you can't stop doing it? | YES / NO |
| Do you wish you did it less or not at all? | YES / NO |

It is possible to overcome all forms of addiction if, deep in your gut, you are ready to confront it head on. Take a look at how you've answered the above. If you've circled YES three times or more, you may be at risk of addiction. There are organizations at the back of the book that can give you specific advice on what you can do about certain unhealthy addictions.

# SELF-HARM

*A bleak epidemic, sweeping silently over a generation. It is in the whispers of classrooms, wrenching guts in our tummies when we think of the things in this world that are hardest to understand.*

39

# WHY WE HURT OURSELVES

Here are some sad and scary statistics about self-harm:

- **One in twelve young people self-harm.**
- **Last year 38,000 young people were admitted to hospital because of their injuries through self-harming.**
- **Hospital admissions due to people self-harming increased by sixty-eight per cent in the last ten years.**

Self-harming is a response to anxiety, fear, chaos and trauma. For self-harmers, it is a coping mechanism and often a shameful secret. We need to deal with the shame factor first and foremost, TALK about self-harm and what lies behind it, and separate the fact from the fiction.

# SELF-HARM: THE MYTHS

During my research for this book, I came across an awesome organization called selfharmUK. Their website is progressive, straight talking and easy to navigate. It lists the important **myths** and **misconceptions** surrounding self-harm, such as:

- **It's only teenagers that self-harm.**
- **People who self-harm are attention-seeking.**
- **Only girls self-harm.**
- **Self-harm only involves cutting.**
- **Self-harm is easy to stop.**
- **Self-harm is a suicide attempt.**
- **Anyone who self-injures is crazy.**
- **Self-harm is a phase and something you just grow out of.**
- **People only self-harm if they've had a really sad life.**

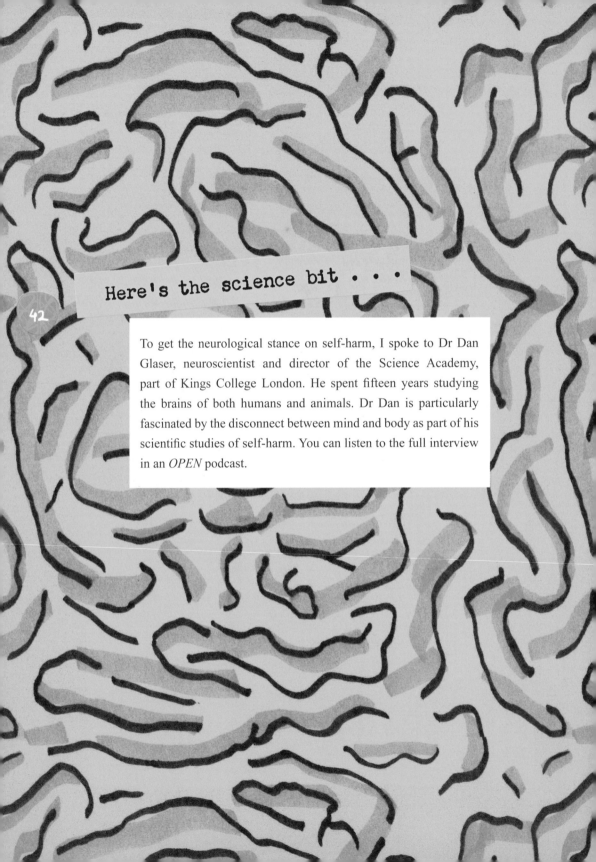

Here's the science bit . . . .

To get the neurological stance on self-harm, I spoke to Dr Dan Glaser, neuroscientist and director of the Science Academy, part of Kings College London. He spent fifteen years studying the brains of both humans and animals. Dr Dan is particularly fascinated by the disconnect between mind and body as part of his scientific studies of self-harm. You can listen to the full interview in an *OPEN* podcast.

66 The first thing to say about it [self-harm] is that it is a paradoxical phenomenon, which is to say it's surprising. Why is it surprising? It's surprising because most of what our brains do, most of our biology, is about maintaining ourselves in good shape. So we sweat when we're hot, we get goose-bumps or shiver when we're cold. When we're thirsty — that's because the salts in our blood are telling our brain we need to drink.

Your whole system of pain in your body is largely designed to stop you from injuring yourself . . . So self-harm is a paradox from a logical point of view because it's an intentional or a deliberate act that goes against your own interests in biology. 99

# GIRLS TALKING ABOUT
## self-harm

As part of a short film project I was producing, I visited a school to talk to teenagers about self-harm. Here I was in the school library, a warm and comforting environment, full of potential.

It was during this hour-long discussion with these teenagers that I learnt more about the deep and lurking issue of self-harm amongst so many young people.

'Self-harm is everywhere.'

'In our year group at school, there's a lot of people that do it.'

'At least three in each class.'

'I feel it has a lot to do with peer pressure. I hear about one person doing it, and then I hear all their friends are doing it — a group is formed.'

## 'Why do you think people are drawn to do it?' I asked.

'Because they want to be popular.'

'A lot of people that do it are from broken homes.'

'So many people tell me they do it, and I don't know what to do.'

## 'So it's a trend?' I ask.

'Yeah. Just type the word "depressed" into Instagram.'

'I'm absolutely terrified at the moment, because of my little sister. She's ten. She's always having arguments with her friends, ya know. She's a complete drama queen, and I'm scared. I'm scared that she might feel the need to do it. If my sister did it, I just don't know what I would do — it's such a horrible thing. And to think that so many people do it. My sister could so easily feel depressed or give in to peer pressure or want to cut herself, because that's what so many people are doing. If this trend keeps going on, it's unavoidable . . .'

So, self-harm amongst teenagers is widespread. It's real and it's scary. But knowing that we are aware and talking about it more is heartening. We need to keep on talking.

# SELF-HARM AND THE ONLINE COMMUNITY

I decide to do some research. When I type certain triggering words into the search box on Instagram, a list of usernames floods my screen, all using the site to visually document their destructive journeys. All the aliases are a variation of each other, each flaunting the fact that they self-harm in their handles, some of which have a tagline labelled 'trigger warning'. I could see how compulsive it must be for some people, how 'catching' these online communities are. For vulnerable people, who desperately need validation, some kind of self-worth, the ease with which they can access the WRONG kind of support rather than portals of advice and help is frightening.

The fact is that self-harming hurts you, and anyone who encourages it is hurting you so much more.

I feel an overwhelming yearning for moderation online. I'm hoping that people know how to handle sites and social networks with care.

I will take this as another opportunity to say please be careful when you are feeling vulnerable. You do not need to be on every social networking site, all of the time. You know if a certain site or user profile is making you feel bad about yourself. It is time to click UNFOLLOW on the stuff that damages us: it feels very powerful and personally liberating to do so.

BE STRONG.

## SELF-HARM: A CASE HISTORY

**I interviewed a brave and beautiful woman – known here as 'A' for 'Anonymous' – who got in touch wanting to open up about her personal experiences with self-harm. Her journey is inspiring and real. You can listen to the podcast interview in full, but here are some powerful words.**

**A:** I've struggled with self-harming since I was about thirteen – so a long, long time. I had a break, and a couple of years ago things started to get really bad. I had a breakdown, and it came back again. It really shocked me. I'm in my thirties and . . . it was like I was a teenager again, and I couldn't manage my feelings; I couldn't cope.

I remember looking for help on self-harm, and I think I was struggling to find anything that related to me at my age. Not just that – it's the shame around self-harm as well . . . It's something that even now I feel ashamed about and scared [to talk] about . . . There's a lot of embarrassment around it. It seems that it's such an extreme form of coping strategy . . . so traumatic and violent, that I couldn't imagine telling anyone what I've done to myself.

I remember scratching myself, and . . . I would cut myself with scissors or a knife, and that happened quite regularly. I was struggling a lot when I was younger, and I took an overdose as well when I'd just turned fourteen. I was just desperate, and after that I continued self-harming for a long, long time. But no one – apart from friends that knew about it – no one really picked up on it. They could see it . . .

**G:** And were there specific things in your life that you were particularly upset about, or was it a more amalgamated mix of dealing with general life and growing up?

**A:** Yeah, I lost my dad when I was really, really young, when I was seven, and . . . that was really difficult . . . On top of being a teenager, fancying boys, being conscious of my body, that was a huge thing. I remember when I was . . . about eight or nine, and looking at myself and thinking, 'If only my legs were smaller.' So it was just this whole mix of growing up as well as what had happened to us as a family . . . If I'd have known, I think, as a teenager, why it was happening, why I was doing it to myself, I think I'd have been able to find ways to cope with things better, and it would've stopped earlier, and I wouldn't have

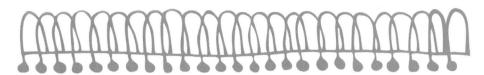

hurt myself so much . . . [If] we share experiences . . . there is a way to kind of deal with it, or to manage it, to get better from it . . . speaking to others and professionals will really help, it will . . .

The feelings still come, and I've got a better way of coping . . . This sounds silly, but I've been trying to make amends with my body. I have scars on my body and they are a constant reminder of times in my life where I've felt completely lost and . . . desperate. But I have to kind of accept my body now and make amends with it . . . I'm . . . now starting my life finally.

**G:** **If you had any tips for anyone, regardless of age – whether they are thirteen or thirty-four – and they can connect with some of the stories that you've told, what would they be?**

**A:** I think the most important thing for me was to talk to people, and to talk to the right people as well – seek professional help. There are so many organizations out there – I got referred to a clinic. They gave me a list of numbers that you can call. I called every one when I was desperate . . .

**G:** **Have you got any recommendations?**

**A:** I spoke to SANE, and there were support groups that I attended. And that was my biggest help, because it was through that that I found out there were a lot of people with eating disorders who self-harmed as a part of that. There's various groups and organizations.

**G:** **It's impossible to be completely sure, but, in your opinion, do you think you would have returned to harming if you'd accessed the right help for you when you were harming when younger?**

**A:** I truly believe if I'd had access to it when younger, hurting myself would not have been a coping strategy for me when I was older. There is help available. To anyone out there struggling with self-harm or emotional issues, you deserve support, you deserve love. Because of the help I received, I survived self-harm, and so will you. So can you. You are not alone. That is the most important thing to remember. You are not alone.

**G:** **OK. Thank you for sharing so much. Thank you, thank you, thank you . . .**

# SELF-HARM:
## GETTING BETTER

We're beginning to understand that, as well as practising caution online, talking about self-harm and exploring the feelings behind it are hugely important in overcoming it. Our feelings and our despair can be overwhelming, but try not to let it create a fog that surrounds you – give yourself time to take a deep breath and consider how to face the issue with perspective rather than harm. Tomorrow is a new day and you are so beautifully precious. Speak up, speak out and be kind to yourself. So many people want you to live a full life and want to help guide you to be happy even if it doesn't always feel like it. I for one am one of those people. So don't be ashamed. If you are self-harming or thinking about it – tell someone immediately and learn to shift the act of self-harm to one of self-care.

# MISSION STATEMENT

**Dear Top Dogs of social media companies and the government,**

It is time. It is time to take a stand. It is time to spend a portion of the money generated from tech innovation on 'tech protection'. I urge you to please accept responsibility for protecting those young, vulnerable and mentally fragile users of your sites by proactively filtering potentially damaging imagery and monitoring submissions to online forums, which are steeped in negative body imagery and promote body harm.

I worry for the young and inquisitive minds, and in my research I realized all too quickly that there isn't enough counterbalance in terms of practical advice and anti-self-harming, body-loathing information. Could there be a strategy put in place? A clearer system that goes beyond the 'report' button? A campaign to explain what you do to protect your users? An in-house 'positivity squad' — monitoring activity of the most harmful sites and users?

Rather than focusing energy on yanking down any picture of a woman's nipples or any sign of menstrual blood — I shout from the rooftops that it is the romanticization of self-harm as a trend that needs to be tackled. It requires boldness and commitment from those in a position of authority to enforce change. We need help and a sense of responsibility alongside these powerful and alluring and often brilliant sites, networks and campaigns.

This needs to be on the agenda — something needs to be done to protect the well-being and mental health of those who spend most of their social life online. The future of tech and social networking needs to be about social consciousness and empowerment, rather than the rampant sense of 'anything goes', which exacerbates bad mental health, creating an epidemic of self-loathing.

It feels like it's become too difficult to tackle, too dark to raise, too scary to mention — but there really is an epidemic amongst young people, and it's time to do something about it.

Yours sincerely,

*Gemma Cairney*

Gemma Cairney

Cut out and send to local MPs and those in a position of power.

# IT'S NOT YOUR FAULT –
# STOP BEATING YOURSELF UP

For those who feel bad about not feeling OK . . .

We All mess up some-times

WE ALL HAVE A DARK SIDE

and sometimes feel in the shade.

# WE ALL CARRY GUILT AND SHAME - SOME-times

I HATE MYSELF. WOe WHY DID I DO SORRY THAT?

How we deal with our dark sides or recover from messing up is the IMPORTANT ISSUE. It is time to stop beating ourselves up for the way we feel and instead OPEN up about our feelings.

You know when you wear a new wool jumper, and you are wishing you'd worn a T-shirt underneath it – but you've realized too late, and you've already stepped out of the house? And it's itching and scratching your bare skin? Making you feel like you're trapped in your own jumper? Making you want to squirm and break free? Guilt and shame can cause your soul to itch in the same way – embedding themselves in your brain in a way that'll make you feel like the jumper can never be taken off.

I think as a society we are excellent at feeling bad about ourselves, obsessing over our worst qualities, when most of us are actually pretty decent human examples. The number of 'guilt-free' products out there implies we should be feeling guilty for everything we usually do. Life is too short to feel guilty about eating cake, that's for sure.

It is worth assessing how often you feel guilt or shame, and whether it balances out with feeling in control and neutral. Work out your patterns of bad feelings – you will either realize how ridiculous it is to apply them to certain things, or accept that if you are doing something that's making you feel genuinely negative, then you need to find some ways to stop doing it.

# YOU ARE NOT alone

The worst thing about feeling down is how lonely and isolated it can make you feel. YOU ARE NOT ALONE. This book and everyone involved in it have unshockable souls – we believe it is never too late, and there are lots of brilliant things for everyone out there. If you are feeling out of control, I urge you to take steps to speak to someone who is trained in hearing your tale. You are not the only one who has felt this way. The sad truth is that many, many others do too. We're gonna have to work together on collectively achieving better mental health in the modern world.

Together, we can be happy and strong.

# The AtoZ

57

## of a Happy Mind

Here is a list of things to try that might pull you out of a dark place. Different things work for different people, so here is a whole alphabet of practical tools, therapy techniques and emotional concepts to consider en route to feeling good in your mind.

**A** **Advice** – get some. There's a list of places you can go for confidential, practical help at the back of this book. **Ashamed:** don't be. **Ask** for help.

**Ambient music.** For some, music can relieve the symptoms of panic. There are albums and albums' worth of ambient music that can literally transcend the most fraught of minds.

**B** **Breaking bad thought patterns.** Do you notice the same things coming into your head all the time? Notice these things, write them down, then think of a positive thought to replace them with.

**C** **Crying** isn't weak or pathetic – it can help you work through your emotions.

**Creativity** can make you feel better – making some art or writing a poem about how you feel can help. You're not alone.

**Communities** exist online for almost anything you're going through – find your people. **Choices:** you have them – even if you feel helpless. **CBT,** or cognitive behavioural therapy, is a brilliant and very popular form of talking therapy that's designed to change our patterns of thought and help us understand why we feel certain things sometimes.

**Counselling** is widely available for free through your GP, and sometimes talking to someone impartial might be what you need. **Chemical imbalance** in your brain might be what's making you feel depressed. If so, medication might help, and there's nothing wrong with that.

**D** **Distractions** can help you get out of your head – find some happy ones. Going to see a doctor can often be a good place to start, to make sure there are no underlying health issues that are affecting your state of mind, and a **diagnosis** might make you see things more clearly. There's NOTHING you can tell them that they won't have heard before.

**E** **Endorphins.** OH YES. I love them. Make them your best friends, sourced the natural way. Stimulate endorphins by moving your body, doing some cartwheels in an open space. Produced by the central nervous system and the pituitary gland, endorphins are essentially happy-makers in our brain.

**Educate** yourself. Seek out information on the way you're feeling.

**Friends and family** – hopefully, amongst them there will be at least one person who will get what you're going through and be able to help. Have a think about who that might be, and arrange to talk to them.

**Get out of the house.** It might be tempting to hide under your duvet until the end of time, and sometimes it might even make you feel a bit better. But, eventually, you have to get out in the world. It's not so bad.

**Healthy habits** and eating. If your mind is a bit unhealthy, then try to keep your body healthy while you work the rest of it out.

**Help others.** This is all about thinking about someone else rather than yourself. When you're feeling bad, it's easy to forget that other people might be worse off than you are.

**Imagination.** Think about the people, places and things that make you happy, and imagine them when you're feeling low.

**Joy.** Find it. Channel it. Remember it.

**Kindness.** Go easy on yourself, above all. Stop punishing yourself for not getting it right all the time. Remember kindness towards other people: an embrace with a friend, a smile at a stranger. Asking someone if they are all right when they have a face full of pain. Kindness is the warmest feeling.

**Laughing** also releases endorphins, and you should do it whenever you can. **Laugh long, laugh loud, laugh often.** A good giddy giggle has been shown to reduce stress hormones. There is even such a thing as laughter therapy. **Laughter therapy** has been shown to have beneficial effects on various aspects of biochemistry. When laughing, the brain releases endorphins that can also relieve physical pain.

**Medication.** There's no stigma in taking it, if it's what's right for you.

**Mindfulness** is a totally free way of finding some peace in your brain and living in the moment. Check out the Headspace app for how to do it.

**Music** can have a powerful effect on your mood – make some happy playlists for when you need a boost.

**N**

**Nourish** your soul and your body; listen to their **needs**. Say **no** to anyone who is dragging you down rather than lifting you up.

**O**

**One thing at a time!** Identify anything that is making you feel bad, make a list and tick them off.

**P**

**Pets** are proven to make us happy.

**Positivity** is SO important. List three things every day that made you feel good, however small. Have **patience** with yourself. Some things take time, and everyone moves at their own pace.

**Psychologists** are best placed to deal with certain problems, and your GP will be able to refer you if they think you would benefit from talking to one.

**Q**

**Quiet** – find somewhere peaceful. If you're an introvert, you might need to take some time alone to feel better. Get away from the noise of the world – that includes social media! Ask **questions** – if you see a GP, a counsellor or any other trained professional, write down anything you want to know and go through it with them. They are there to answer any questions you might have.

**R**

**Read** – reading books is the most enriching escapism there is.

**Relax** in the best way you know how. Whether it's watching TV, reading, having a bath, gardening or hanging out with your friends – do it regularly. Let your shoulders drop, breathe deeply and relax.

**Reflect** – don't always look ahead, but breathe deep in the present, and reflect on the past.

**Support** – can be found in the right places.

**Space** – make some in your brain.

**Smell**. I love the idea that fragrance and aromatherapy can be a 'go-to' for a busy mind. Bergamot and eucalyptus are advised for 'emotional exhaustion', for example, as is ginger for 'intellectual fatigue'. A fantastic book about this, and more, is *The Fragrant Mind: Aromatherapy for Personality, Mind and Emotion* by Valerie Ann Worwood, 1996.

**Talk** about it, **tell** someone, seek **therapy**.

**Understand** your triggers.

**Vent**. Shout and scream if you need to, to someone who understands you.

**Walk** it out and **write** it down – take time and space with your thoughts, and they might sort themselves into some sort of order you can understand.

**XOXO**. Kissing the right person can make you feel more rooted to the planet than anything you can do with another human being.

**Yoga**. Get bendy and feel more in control of your body.

**Zzzzzz** . . . get enough sleep! Sleep is soul power.

# READING LIST FOR MENTAL HEALTH

Some great, inspirational books that deal with mental health are listed below.

***She's Come Undone*** by Wally Lamb

***Mind Your Head*** by Juno Dawson

***Undone*** by Cat Clarke

***Mealtimes and Milestones: A Teenager's Diary of Moving on from Anorexia*** by Constance Barter

***Understanding Teenage Depression*** by Maureen Empfield

***The Brain – The Story of You*** by David Eagleman

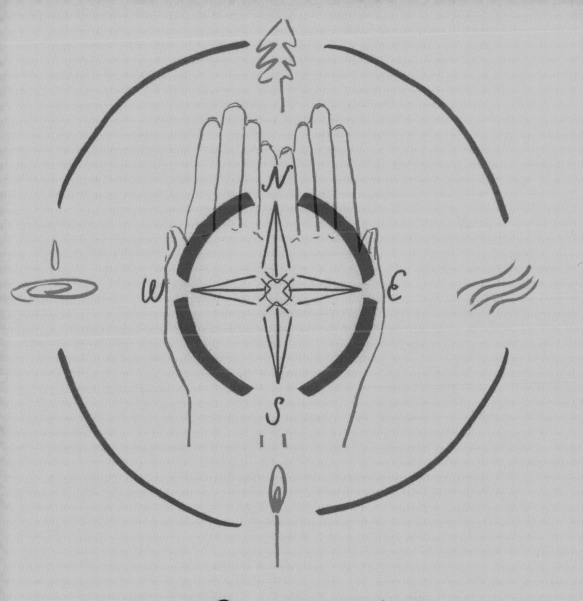

YOUR WORLD
AND
YOUR FUTURE

# INTRODUCTION

Think about the world – your globe. Picture it in your head: its roundness – the swirls of delicious greens and blues of the land and seas and oceans. Think about those continents you learn about in geography lessons – how they become so easily identifiable from their beautiful shapes. Think about all the islands in their thousands and thousands. Think about how BIG the world is – all the places you've been, and all the places you would like to see in the future.

Now think about you. Where are you on that globe right now, while you're reading these words?

This part of *Open Your Mind* looks at what it means to be a human being, to see what's important about it, what's sad about it, what's truly joyful about it. And how, even though we only physically occupy the tiniest little patch of the world at any given time, we can add something HUGE to it . . . We can add boundless love and hope, in an infinite number of ways.

The world is EXTRAORDINARY. It can sometimes be gut-sickeningly sad and terrifying, but it's also ridiculously fun and boldly beautiful . . . EXTRAORDINARY. Your world is your future.

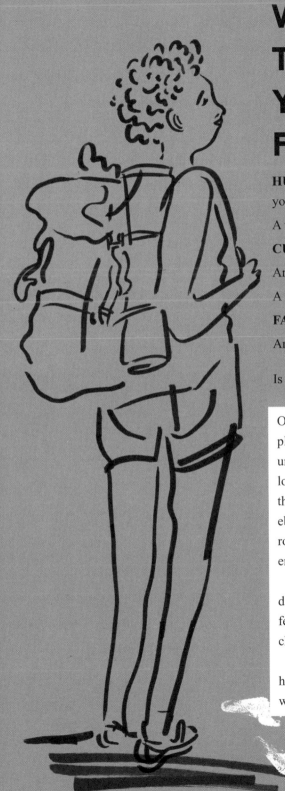

# WHAT YOU NEED TO PACK IN YOUR RUCKSACK FOR THIS TRIP

**HUMILITY** – the ability to be humble and leave your vanity at the door.

A willingness to **LISTEN**.

**CURIOSITY** and the confidence to ask questions.

An understanding of **ACTIVISM** over **ANGER**.

A sense of **WONDER** for nature.

**FASCINATION** and bewilderment combined.

An **OPEN** heart and **OPEN** mind.

Is your bag packed? LET'S GO . . .

Our world can sometimes seem like an overwhelming place to be: sometimes scary, sometimes bleak, often unfair. But with every low there is a high. To understand love, you must understand the opposite; to enjoy the sun, there must be shade. But even when we feel at our lowest ebb, there are never-ending, awe-inspiring experiences round every corner if we find a way to tap into our great energy reserves and just get out there and find them.

One of our biggest problems with the world is how disconnected we sometimes feel from it. It is hard to feel rooted to a general environment that is constantly changing and sometimes feels out of our control.

But it's not out of our control: we have a voice, hopes and dreams, and a sense of what's right and wrong . . . Please keep going.

# POLITICS

Politics in the UK can seem like a lot of boring posh people shouting at each other in the House of Commons – that big, dark, heavy room, void of all natural light, with its gloomy green leather-clad seats, and its opulent, Gothic architecture. It is all too easy for the heckles, the angry faces and the strange language to make politics feel difficult to understand, hard to connect to and too remote from the reality of our day-to-day lives – as though it has no relevance.

But it does . . . It REALLY does. A lot of what politicians and the government are deciding now, the laws they are putting in place, will affect your future – your livelihood, your ability to buy a house, even your access to a functioning health service.

I will never, ever forget being lucky enough to be shown round the chamber of the House of Commons by an MP. He scurried about excitedly, as though he was showing off his impressive gaff on MTV *Cribs*! (Anyone remember that show? It basically gave us a peek round super-famous people's insane houses. Google 'Mariah Carey Cribs' to watch a classic episode.) I bought a bottle of 'House of Commons' – branded champagne for twenty-five quid from the gift shop – because I thought it was ludicrous that it existed – and marvelled at the colossal size of everything.

As I walked around, I was moved to think of the brave ones in this world. I bowed my head at a plaque dedicated to Nelson Mandela in Westminster Hall; and I thought of the many young women before me who dedicated their lives to fighting for women to gain the right to vote. Women like Emily Wilding Davison (who allegedly once hid in a crypt in the very burrows we were being shown around), who, in June 1913, was struck when she walked out in front of the King's horse during the Epsom Derby race to draw attention to the seriousness of the suffragette movement, and later died in hospital from her injuries (it is still unknown whether it was intended martyrdom).

I was shown the chambers where MPs go when they have to make big decisions about the laws of the land. My guide told me that one particularly momentous day of parliamentary decision-making was when MPs decided on the legal maximum number of weeks at which a woman should still be permitted to have an abortion. It was at that moment it truly struck – like lightning – just how much power this lot has in all our lives . . . right down to the things that feel the most intense and most personal.

You have to be eighteen years old in this country to be able to vote, but it's never too early to start learning more about politics and how you can get involved as you get closer to voting age. Try to work out whether you are left wing, right wing or somewhere in between. See the back of this book for some great organizations that are ace in engaging us normal folk when it comes to politics. Knowing what your choices are is empowering and helpful when it comes to casting your vote, which, by the way, is one of the most important things you will EVER do in your adult life. PLEASE VOTE. We all have the right: people fought for that, so use it. According to recent electoral reform statistics, one in four eighteen to twenty-one-year-olds had not registered to vote. This is not good! Particularly when you consider that in the 1960s over seventy per cent of eighteen to twenty-four-year-olds voted. Now, I'm FULLY aware that the boring admin effort that seems to be involved in registering might not be your priority over all the other things you've got to get sorted. Just know that if you're not voting, then you are not changing all the things that will affect you, and many others like you, the most: our homes, the environment, health care and money. You can do something about that. Take a bit of time to think about what you want from our political system. A younger voice in this country is what's lacking – so use yours.

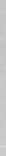

# POLITICS
## HOW DOES IT MAKE YOU FEEL?

**ANGRY?**

Head to page 71 for more on how you can convert anger into activism.

**CONFUSED?**
But want to do more?

Go to www.bitetheballot.co.uk to learn how you can become an active change-maker.

Head to page 71 for tips from a former MP on how to get into politics.

**EMPOWERED?**
And would love to know how to get into politics further?

**OVER-WHELMED?**

Go to www.bitetheballot.co.uk to learn how you can become an active change-maker.

**MEH?**

No power, so it doesn't concern you. Do you use public transport? Do you watch *EastEnders*? Do you get a doctor or hospital appointment for free? Do you pay tax? If you can answer yes to any of those, then it does concern you. Go to www.bitetheballot.co.uk to learn how you can become an active change-maker.

**EXCITED?**
And politically engaged? Read on!

Go to www.bitetheballot.co.uk to learn how you can become an active change-maker.

# A SIMPLE BREAKDOWN OF POLITICAL TERMS

**Anarchism:** Anarchists believe that the state and forms of compulsory government are harmful or unnecessary to people's lives.

**Communism:** Communists believe that the capitalist system is damaging to the interests of the masses, and that workers must unite to overthrow it.

**Conservatism:** Conservative thinking originates in the belief that traditional institutions and modes of government that have evolved over time function the best, and that political change should be organic and not revolutionary.

**Environmentalism:** Believes in protecting and improving the condition of the natural environment, including greater regulation of human interaction with it, as well as those aspects of our lives that are environmentally unsustainable and damaging.

**Feminism:** Feminists seek full equality in political, social and economic spheres in order to redress the balance in a society and political system that is considered to be patriarchal (run by men!).

**Left-wing politics:** Usually progressive in nature, left-wing beliefs look to the future, aim to support those who cannot support themselves, are idealist and believe in equality. People who are left-wing believe in taxation to redistribute opportunity and wealth. Institutions like the NHS and the welfare state (e.g. jobseeker's allowance) are fundamentally left-wing ideas.

**Liberalism:** Liberals believe in protecting the rights of the individual to ensure their maximum freedom – and that civil liberties and freedoms must be safeguarded and protected by the state.

**Right-wing politics:** These beliefs value tradition, are about equity, survival of the fittest and economic freedom. Right-wing beliefs espouse that business shouldn't be regulated and that freedom for individuals to succeed is paramount over equality.

**Socialism:** Socialists are motivated to improve the quality of life for every member of society – and believe in the redistribution of resources (including money) to redress inequalities in a free-market economy.

VOTE

# THE ACTIVIST

I got advice from **Jo Swinson**, Lib Dem MP and former government minister and author of *Equal Power*, on how to get involved with changing things that affect you, and those around you:

Voting is important, but there's much more to politics, and lots that you can do even before you're old enough to vote. You can **raise issues with the people elected to represent you** - enter your postcode at **www.theyworkforyou.com** and you'll get the full list of who they are. Email them about the issues you care about or, even better, check when they are holding an 'advice surgery' and go along - this is where you can chat to them face to face, often in a local library or town hall. And campaign to build support for the issues you care about - any UK citizen can **start a petition to parliament.**

Political parties bring together people who share similar ideas about what needs to change. **Joining a party** is a great way to learn about campaigning, and by working with other people your efforts are more likely to make a difference. You can find out about what parties believe on their websites and social media accounts, and by watching programmes like BBC *Question Time*. You don't need to agree one hundred per cent with everything a party says to join, and it's usually only a few pounds for young people, so choose the one that is closest to your views and go for it! And **you're never too young** . . . I was elected as an MP at twenty-five, and in 2015 Mhairi Black was elected as an MP at the age of twenty.

# TALKING POLITICS

I asked Josie Long, comedian and co-founder of charity Arts Emergency (whose aim is to ensure the doors of the university are kept open for those most able to benefit from but least able to pay for education) why she thinks it's important to be politicized, and how popular culture and the arts have a definite role to play in humanizing politics.

**GC:** Why do you think that a lot of people just shy away from politics altogether?

**JL:** It's definitely easier to not care about it . . . to be complacent. I also think if you're explicitly political, if you pick a side in anything, especially if you come out as anti the status quo a little bit, you're making a real choice in some ways to have people disagree with you and judge you. That can negatively impact your life. I definitely think I've probably lost work because of it, or had arguments with people because of it. But to care about politics is to just care: care about the most wonderful parts of life — and because you think everyone deserves wonderful things. So you care from a position of real joy and love. But sometimes it's easier to think, 'Ya know what — I don't want to have a go at my nice parents who voted in a way I wouldn't.' Or, 'Not everyone who disagrees with me is bad'. . . blah blah blah. So then you can reduce how vocal you are on certain things.

**GC:** I think that politics affects our emotional well-being — what do you think?

**JL:** It's interesting, politics, because some people do not have the luxury of choosing whether or not they're involved. If you get kicked out of your council home, it's not a choice. There are so many things like that where it will affect you and hurt you — it comes into your life, and then you have to deal with it. I totally agree with you that the wider sphere of politics impacts on all people . . . Look at climate change — 'Why are the seasons [going] wrong?' Every five minutes you have a conversation with someone where you go, 'This summer's been really weird.' On a deep-rooted level, it's all connected to our political system.

**GC:** But then when you turn on the telly and you try to understand the news . . . I feel like it's so unrelatable that it's hard to know what to do, and can often render you pretty helpless.

72

**JL:** The way the modern world operates — especially with politics — is it convinces you that you're stupid and you know nothing, and it's not for you . . . It's very easy to feel like there's this amorphous mass, and you couldn't possibly do anything. On a local level, a lot of things that used to be participatory community political things have gone. People have to find their communities online or in a more global sense. It's more and more sprawling, so it's harder. The good thing about it is it's a really easy thing to find again. If you scratch the surface in this country, there's people getting on with stuff that you'll be in awe of everywhere, and they need you more than ever. There's volunteer groups, there's community groups, there's activist groups, there's arts groups, there's everything. There's really good groups like Citizens UK, which is the home of community organizing in the UK.

**GC:** How important is art when it comes to politics?

**JL:** Incredibly so. Think about creativity and critical thought. So, critical thought is obviously the ability to question and the ability to examine; and creativity is the ability to imagine and think up new things and make them. That is how to understand society better, and to be useful to society: understanding what's going on, addressing problems and solving them. I think creativity's massively important for politics. On a very basic level, it lets you imagine something better . . . It's good to know what direction you're pointing in. There's no one that doesn't deserve to be looked after in our society, and there's no one in our society that doesn't deserve to be a fully fledged citizen — even if they're unemployed — everywhere in this country should be habitable.

**GC:** What do you do if you don't agree with your best friend or your parents when it comes to politics? How the hell are you supposed to still get on?

**JL:** Try to be generous. When it comes down to it, try to put your view across. I think it's very important to learn about how people derail you in arguments, because people love to play devil's advocate — they try to provoke you — and what's quite nice is that you are not necessarily obliged to defend yourself all the time. If you believe things politically, you don't always have to be explaining why. You can just say, 'I have a right to my opinion.'

# MELTING POT OF MAD

We live in unbelievably unsettling times. The world over, the unpredictability of how people vote and the actions of others makes me wonder whether the world has lost sight of human kindness. It makes me feel mashed up and tangled inside, raging mad and sad in the pit of my stomach.

I felt saddened and maddened when I heard that a group of young black men in a workshop (held by my performance-artist friend Bryony Kimmings) said that they felt powerless in our political system. I still feel mad from the day that I visited the place where suffragette Emily Wilding Davison (mentioned earlier in the 'Politics' section) was trampled to death by the King's horse in 1913, whilst fighting for votes for women.

I am mad about what I learned when I made a documentary for BBC3 in 2011 about the riots that had set alight some of the UK's major cities the summer before. I am mad and sad for lives ruined, for all those affected in a spiralling mess that largely came from opportunism, materialism and social media rampancy, and an underlying exasperation towards the system. I am mad for the families of those killed in the many acts of terrorism around the world, sickeningly too many to mention. I am sad and mad that the blazing magic-bearers David Bowie and Prince died in 2016. It is impossible not to want to cry every time I am informed of more tragic world news.

. . . And yet the beat goes on. We are a generation more connected and enabled by technology. We will live longer than generations before us. We need to work out what we can do. How can we turn our sadness into action? How can we learn to protest peacefully, educate ourselves so we don't feel so politically powerless and create positive change? Every time I hear of injustice or tragedy – every time I see another repulsive, attention-seeking opportunist shouting and spouting rage and hatred online – it makes me want to stomp out the shoot of despair it creates inside me, and instead plant a seed of warmth and love, which can grow and spread joy in its place.

One thing I do know is that no one should ever, EVER combat violence with violence. The sweetest revenge of all is LOVE. Love is the most powerful thing on this planet. Perhaps we need to turn off regular newsfeeds on our devices and only delve into news about the world's disasters and sadness when we feel like we are ready to do so. I feel there is a balance to be struck between staying informed and protecting our own mental health.

We must remember it is not all doom and gloom, even when we are at our most fearful. Being mindful of the sheer number of joy-filled happenings that occur on this planet can help us combat even the most horrific news. Seek that joy, that goodness, out. A sunset will always be beautiful; an embrace will always bring warmth and safety. Plus there are some phenomenal people in the world doing phenomenal things for good. Be one of them.

## A checklist for living in this political world

☐ It is OK to cry. It is OK to be angry. But learn to channel this into something spectacular.

☐ Discuss, ask questions and educate yourself.

☐ Use your right to vote.

☐ As long as the world still exists, there will always be hope. Go find it.

☐ Remember how important you are – you are great . .

You – yes you – can change the world.

# EXPERIENCE

We each experience life uniquely. The most important thing is to find our own voice, and learn how to use it – this is invaluable, regardless of political stance. To feel rooted like a tree in your loves, your dislikes and your wants for your world is a way of affirming your place in it. I asked writer Frances Acquaah, from South London, to open up and write about her world and experiences.

# #NOFILTER
## by Frances Acquaah

I pretty much had my whole life planned out growing up — putting age stamps on future life milestones. By twenty-eight I was going to own my dream house before being swept off my feet by Prince Charming. After having children (including at least one set of twins), we would build our empire, travel the world and retire early.

Needless to say, life has happened, and any hope of the above coming true is as mythical as the fairy-tale ending I had imagined. At least not any time soon. I do still possess hope, though.

Though it does feel like we are all pretty much doomed on the dream-house front . . . especially if you live in a city.

A report by Aviva predicts that by 2025 a third of young adults will have to move back into their childhood bedroom.

At the end of the day, none of the main parties are doing anything in the interest of young people. None of them are fighting our corner; they are too busy throwing shade at each other in parliament, and only care to give us a second thought when it's campaign time. That's how it seems, anyway.

I was the first person from my immediate family to go to university. I didn't really see it as an achievement at the time, because my Sixth Form made it seem like it was the next natural step — there was no other option. Now I am waist deep in thousands of pounds of debt, and although I made some lifelong friends it is far from worth it.

Like many, when I left university I felt a sense of entitlement and pride; I thought I was too good for retail, and I definitely wasn't going to sign on. Getting a degree meant access to better, higher-paid jobs — so I had been told. It was a very humbling experience when I had to return back to the shop floor, to say the least. Somehow, six months later, I managed to land myself a job in a role that was actually relevant to my degree. Luckily, I've been working in the media industry ever since.

In this financial climate, not everyone has been as fortunate as myself, and many graduates have had to put their dream career on hold in order to survive, working in admin, recruitment agencies or call centres — just some of the more popular roles graduates tend to take on so they can escape retail.

When I was working as an editor of a youth magazine, some of the younger contributors taught me some of the unwritten rules for Instagram. The one that stuck and shocked me the most was the 'one-like-per-minute rule'. Apparently, once you have uploaded a picture, if you don't get at least one like per minute, it means your picture isn't going to 'perform well' — so many young people will just delete it out of embarrassment.

This is their reality; this is where we are.

I see myself as a bit of a piggy in the middle. I'm in a unique position where the internet is second nature, but still I would give it up in a heartbeat if it was a choice between that and natural daylight.

Unfortunately, many of us place our value on how many 'likes' we get and how many people are following us across our social media. So many young people (and adults) are chasing ideals of beauty that only exist after multiple filters have been applied, and we are allowing brands to capitalize every day on insecurities we didn't even know we had.

There are people doing gymnastics so the lens can capture their red-bottom shoes all for the validation of people they have never met! And I'm not saying it's bad to have expensive things, but you can't say you don't care what people think of you on one hand, but then say you can't wear an outfit because you've previously posted it on social media.

Oh, and let's not forget hashtag [insert] goals — from someone else's body, to their relationships, to what they had for breakfast. It's exhausting.

We've barely touched the surface with regards to research on the links between social media and mental health. Like you'll never know how my fourteen-year-old cousin laughed in my face when he saw my Snapchat score — I didn't realize it was a competition. You'll only be aware of the true extent of it all if you are on the ground.

In order to overcome FOMO, we can't be constantly glued to our phones. It's so important to use everything in balance. Let your social media be an extension of your truth, and learn to love what you see when you look at yourself without the filters.

The decisions you make about your life will affect you in the long run, no one else. Take in every moment in the present and enjoy it; it's not necessary to Snapchat it all the time.

# GENERATION DIY

The government's lack of concern for young people means that we have had no option but to create our own opportunities.

One good thing that has risen from our lack of prospects is the number of start-ups driven by young people. A study by Hays revealed that the majority of Generation Y viewed the idea of becoming an entrepreneur attractive, with sixty-one per cent either having their own business or interested in running one in the future.

Initially dubbed a 'lazy generation', we have proven that we are in fact the complete opposite: ambitious, business savvy and innovative — they should consider renaming us 'Generation DIY'.

# OUR NATURAL WORLD

Our environment sometimes seems a little poorly, doesn't it? You can feel it in the air when we experience erratic weather – wetter, windier winters . . . drier, more sweltering summers. And when we learn of natural disasters around the world, like the fierce hurricanes that savage towns and ravage people's lives, our hearts ache at our sense of powerlessness.

BUT we all have the potential to help. When thinking about our environment, is it important to know that if we collectively become more conscious of what we can do to protect it then it could be possible to halt a lot of environmental damage, just by introducing small changes into our day-to-day lives.

But we need to do it TOGETHER. Ignite passion for our planet!

# EIGHT SIMPLE WAYS TO DO YOUR BIT

1 Reduce. Reuse. Recycle. If you don't recycle your rubbish, then WHY don't you? If you live with your parents or in a shared house that hasn't got into recycling, then you be the ONE that starts, and get everyone else to do it too.

2 Take it a step further and start a compost heap (compost is decayed organic material used as fertilizer to grow plants). Most local councils can provide you with a composting bin to get you on your merry green serene way.

3 When you have a special event that you are buying an outfit for, think about ethical and eco-friendly clothing. Research the brands that make beautiful clothes without exploiting people or the environment, and you can get yourself an ethically sound outfit. Or the next time you are buying a new pair of shoes, think about where you get them from. Beyond Skin, for example, make bangingly brilliant vegan faux-leather shoes.

4 Go for a spree in your local charity shop (I have honestly found some of my greatest purchases in charity shops – including a full tweed suit, a fluorescent-yellow ski jacket and a Hollywood-worthy faux-fur grizzly-bear-brown coat).*

5 Get a washing line if you don't have one already; tumble dryers guzzle energy at a monstrous rate.

6 Grow your own vegetables. Even if you don't have a garden, you can invest in a vegetable growbag. They are wicked for balconies, patios and small front gardens. The joy of growing is too humungous to ignore. (Head to page 86 for more on plants.)

7 Get a beehive!! (More on this on pages 82–84.)

8 Sign up to the Greenpeace newsletter to stay informed on the globe, its challenges and how we can help.

*If you successfully buy a brilliant outfit from a charity shop that you adore, please take a snap and share it, tagging me @gemagain, and announcing that you're #TeamOpen. I wanna see all the immense charity-shop bargains!

# NATURAL HOBBIES

BELIEVE IT OR NOT, not *everything* fun is to be found online. Did you know there are so many things we can do that don't cost much money and don't involve a keyboard or a screen . . . just our natural resources and the wonderful world around us?

Bees do it better.

Bees – what beguiling and fascinating creatures they are, not only the inspiration for the colour scheme of *Open*, being yellow and black, but genuinely vital to our environment too.

I interviewed Becca, a fifteen-year-old beekeeper, to find out more about this essential and illuminating badass hobby.

Local Honey

**GC:** I believe that we as humans could learn from bee life. Would you agree?

**B:** Yeah, bees are what people describe as a super-organism: every bee in the hive has a job. One thing I find very interesting about bees is that when they sting you they will die — but they're not doing it because they feel frightened; they do it because they feel their colony is endangered. They're not selfish at all, which I really find quite cool. Another interesting fact is that the majority of the bees in the hive are girl bees. It's a peculiar fact, but the boy bees are only there to mate with a new queen . . . this is their only reason to be. In the winter, the girl bees kick them out of the hive. The girl bees are the more important ones.

**GC:** How has beekeeping changed your life?

**B:** The best thing that beekeeping's done for me is created loads of opportunities. I've gone across Europe with bees, and I've talked to other people from all over the world, where we have different backgrounds but such a common interest — beekeeping. It's a nice thing to bond over.

**GC:** People out there might think, 'Oh, I live somewhere where I just couldn't have a hive,' or, 'This just isn't for me.' Are there ways of making it work in a city?

**B:** You don't really have to have a large amount of land: I know of people that keep bees on roofs of buildings. It's really quite easy to keep them in most areas.

**GC:** How does beekeeping enhance your life?

**B:** I personally think it's great and everybody should learn about it, because it makes you look at the world from a different point of view. You suddenly start to think, 'Well, without bees we wouldn't have this, or we wouldn't have that.' It's a constant reminder that they're such an important part of our world.

**GC:** Have you been stung before?

**B:** Yep. Normally I try not to get stung because it hurts, but it does occasionally happen.

**GC:** I went to Ethiopia in East Africa with Oxfam, and I met with beekeepers there living in tiny villages, who were changing the face of their communities by gaining an income from making and then selling honey. The fact that the women would do it from home, bring up families and beekeep was perfect for their lifestyles. Would you be interested in travelling around the world and finding out more about beekeeping?

**B:** Definitely. There is an organization called Bees Abroad, and they go to developing countries. I was speaking to somebody the other day, and they said that there was girl who paid for her education all the way up to university through keeping bees.

**GC:** It's a really beautiful way of connecting to others and our natural world.

**B:** Yeah. Me, my sister and my dad beekeep together, and my mum helps bottle all the honey — it is a real family thing. We also take our bees to do demonstrations and chat to the public.

**GC:** So for those that don't know, how does it improve the world to look after bees?

**B:** Without beekeepers, honeybees wouldn't be able to survive in this country because there are certain diseases and pests which will kill them off. So what we're doing is we're helping them survive, which helps pollinate plants, giving us fruits and flowers and a happier, healthier environment.

**GC:** And a constant supply of honey. We can't dismiss THAT — that is so good!

**B:** Quite a lot of my friends keep saying, 'Becca, can I have a jar of honey?' It is really nice, because it's a standalone thing, which only I do . . . It's really interesting, and it makes me different from everybody else. I like that in a way. I like being different.

# PLANTS

Pssssssssssssssssssstttttttt. It's fun to go potty with planting. It makes your insides smile to nurture a living thing. It automatically roots you to nature. Whether it's a miniature cactus or a glorious, giant *Oxalis triangularis* – aka the butterfly plant . . . aka purple shamrocks – fill your house and surround yourself with them. There are thousands of videos on YouTube giving advice on how to look after specific plants.

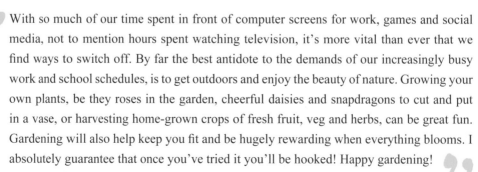

With so much of our time spent in front of computer screens for work, games and social media, not to mention hours spent watching television, it's more vital than ever that we find ways to switch off. By far the best antidote to the demands of our increasingly busy work and school schedules, is to get outdoors and enjoy the beauty of nature. Growing your own plants, be they roses in the garden, cheerful daisies and snapdragons to cut and put in a vase, or harvesting home-grown crops of fresh fruit, veg and herbs, can be great fun. Gardening will also help keep you fit and be hugely rewarding when everything blooms. I absolutely guarantee that once you've tried it you'll be hooked! Happy gardening!

*Rachel de Thame, gardener and presenter on BBC Two's* Gardeners' World

86

# TREES

Just as bees are super important for our natural environment, so are trees. Trees are the most dynamic natural resource we have. Not only do they look like glorious, wise old creatures – they also clean the air we breathe by absorbing pollutants and generating oxygen. Those lovely special trees, they create habitats for wildlife, helping species to survive and thrive. They provide protection from weather extremes and prevent surface water flooding. They transform our landscapes. They are a part of our history and national identity. They are good for our health – research has found that people who live in greener areas experience lower levels of mental distress and have a better quality of life. What is not to LOVE about trees?

We can do our bit to keep our trees growing and thriving. We need to stand up for them as they are under constant threat from redevelopment. Find out what is happening to large areas of tree-filled green around where you live. If there are redevelopment plans for any of them, then write to your local council and your MP (more on how you can do this on page 71). Tell your friends to do the same. Volunteer for the Woodland Trust, who are dedicated to the protection of our native trees and woodlands. Get involved! Now go and give a tree a hug, at the risk of sounding insane I have tried this a few times and it feels bizarrely joyous.

The ability to communicate is liberating and cool, so load up with the good words, learn them – let them wrap around you and protect you. Fill your heart and mind with the tools of talking. Arm yourself with your beautiful language. Words empower you. Words make life more interesting and beautiful too. A good vocabulary is enriching – a brilliant tool for creativity.

Play the word puzzle below, and see which words you can identify with.

```
              S W W C              H S W Q
          F V W B J G          O D E O M M
        R A I E X D I Q      B G M V W K P I
      N E N N D A I V I A G E F T I D X P B X
    Z Y H T Z R C F K F F N J C V S V N O Y N T
  J V N T A U A I F A J I I D A C S J M L K P N Y
  X D E O S K G M E B D S R T I A E G U E A Q A R
  I O W R T W E I R D O G E N D L R N G N C X I D
  U M P F I E S C E O D M E B I T G L T O S X L I
  X Y F R C F D P N B Y Y N V O E O L J R K O L C
  C Z L Z A S A K T Q O E O D S R R T W C I J I X
    A E P L E W A M U O M I D Y N P C E A F C R
    E T V Y A S H S I E K P J N A P N G V C X B
      S N I X C T R R M K W S C T H I A A N E
        N M T F I S K P N M J R I T T Z N V
          T Q A X D Y X V F J A V U S H T
          G Z V U A U C L I T E V I R
          Z K O M R U A A I G Z D
            E Q N W J H I C A U
            Y X N S V V L M
              G C I B G Y
              M N O Y
              X Q
```

96

| ALTERNATIVE | DISTINCT | IDIOSYNCRATIC | PROGRESSIVE |
|---|---|---|---|
| AVANT | ECCENTRIC | INNOVATIVE | QUIRKY |
| BRILLIANT | FANTASTICAL | OTHER | RADICAL |
| DIFFERENT | GARDE | PIONEERING | |

**Alternative:** 1) one or more things available as another possibility or choice and 2) relating to activities that depart from or challenge traditional norms

**Avant garde:** original or innovative (especially with reference to popular music)

**Brilliant:** 1) very bright light or colour and 2) exceptionally clever or talented

**Different:** 1) not the same as another or each other, unlike in nature, form or quality and 2) distinct, separate

**Distinct:** 1) recognizably different in nature from something else of similar type and 2) readily distinguishable by the senses

**Eccentric:** 1) unconventional and slightly strange person and 2) not placed centrally, or not having its axis or other part placed centrally

**Fantastical:** 1) conceived or appearing as conceived by an unrestrained imagination and 2) odd, bizarre, grotesque

**Idiosyncratic:** relating to idiosyncracy – peculiar or individual

**Innovative:** 1) relating to a product, idea, etc., one featuring new methods and 2) advanced and original

**Other:** 1) used to refer to a person or thing that is different or distinct from one already mentioned and 2) further, additional

**Pioneering:** involving new ideas or methods

**Progressive:** 1) happening or developing gradually or in stages and 2) of a person or idea, favouring social reform

**Quirky:** having or characterized by peculiar or unexpected traits or aspects

**Radical:** 1) (especially of change or action) relating to or affecting the fundamental nature of something and 2) characterized by departure from tradition, innovative or progressive

# THE INTERNET

The other world we increasingly inhabit is the worldwide web. The internet is a good place to find your tribe, your community and people with similar ideals – through platforms, blogs and online discussion forums. It's great for catching up with friends and family members who live around the world. It's hilarious for goats that sound as if they are talking! It's bad for browsing or stalking – how much time is spent looking at trousers or our ex's new partner? It's horrific for the amount of lies and death and doom it fills your brain with. It's toxic, with evil people trying to get you to spend money to talk to them. It's ugly when people are mean. It's dangerously obsessive.

There are as many bits to the internet world as there are to the real one. Living in TWO WORLDS is EXHAUSTING! In order not to let it 'cage us' we should load ourselves with the knowledge of its potential and face up to how it can affect us, for better or worse. This involves embracing the fantastic side of tech innovation, but also it means treating the internet the same way as we would anything that is bad for our health or that we could get addicted to – RESPONSIBLY. ALSO acquaint yourself with the power of the plug. The plug is as powerful as a lightsaber against negativity, and YOU have the power to switch the internet off, whenever you want. That 'off' button is your friend and, thankfully, there's loads of other fun things to do in life.

# SIX DIZZYING INTERNET FACTS

**1** In China there are treatment camps for internet addicts. Two hundred million internet users in China are between the ages of fifteen and thirty-five, and that demographic is seen as the most 'likely' to lose self-control. Tao Ran, director of the country's first internet-addiction treatment clinic in Beijing, said that forty per cent of those addicted to the internet suffer from attention deficit hyperactivity disorder, also known as ADHD.

**2** According to common folklore, the first emoticon was created by a bloke called Kevin MacKenzie in 1979 and looked like . . . drum roll, pleeeeease . . . this:  -)

**3** It is estimated that eighty per cent of all images on the internet are of naked women.

**4** For a period in 2013, the first autofill that would pop up if you typed 'Is it legal to' was 'own a sloth?'. Yep, 'Is it legal to own a sloth?' At the time of writing this book, the first thing that comes up is, 'Is it legal to marry your cousin?' Ermmm . . .

**5** A very brainy physicist called Russell Seitz has worked out that the ENTIRE internet weighs approximately as much as one single strawberry.

**6** Every sixty seconds over seventy-two hours of YouTube content is uploaded. That's too much to keep on top of, I reckon.

# THE INTERNET
## (THE WORLDWIDE WEB)

## THE GOOD STUFF

**There are SO MANY benefits to using the internet.** Things like connectivity – the amount of people you can stay in touch with now; globalization; **self-education** – *click*, *click*, *click*. So much amazing information is readily there for us. Finding like-minded others is awesome – your scene, your community. And one of the greatest things the internet does is facilitate **self-exploration** – you can play with your identity online in a way that you can't play with it offline.

So the internet is an amazingly good thing in so many ways. From finding long-lost friends, to researching for your studies, to having an amazing fun-filled chat with your best mate who lives far away. Skype, FaceTime, they keep us close when we can't physically be with someone. The likes of Instagram can bring out the creativity in us and share it. It can make you feel less alone. It can make you smile. So far so good.

## THE STUFF THAT CAN HURT US

With the help of Dr Alison Attrill-Smith, senior lecturer in Cyber Psychology at the University of Wolverhampton, who heads up one of the biggest cyber psychology research groups in the UK, we came up with this comprehensive guide of what we need to be aware of, wary of and responsible for when it comes to the internet.

## BOUNDARIES

A boundary is the line marking the limits of an area, and boundaries are usually in place for a good reason. Research proves that the **boundaries of internet use** are becoming very flexible when it comes to how younger people behave online. One of the obvious examples is revenge porn, which many people access and use without realizing it is wrong.

*Revenge porn is the sharing of private sexual materials, either photos or videos, of another person without their consent and with the purpose of causing embarrassment or distress.*

*Revenge porn is a new offence, recognized by UK law, that applies both online and offline and to images which are shared electronically or in a more traditional way, so it includes the uploading of images on the internet, sharing by text or email, or showing someone a physical or electronic image.*

*If you are worried about anything regarding this subject, head to www.revengepornhelpline.org.uk*

## YOUR DIGITAL FOOTPRINT

People think they're anonymous online. They are not. In the early stages of internet communication, people *were* anonymous, but that's no longer the case. It's so easy to find someone's true identity – their digital footprint – online. It's important to remember this before you post anything. Ask yourself, ***'Would I say this in the real world? Would I want my family to see this?'*** Even if you delete something quickly, the thing about online posts is that they never really go away. Within seconds, someone may have screen-grabbed it, or may at least remember it. Your actions can have huge consequences online.

94

Technology records things, IP addresses, etc. You are never anonymous online nowadays. So just think about what you're putting online. The danger is sharing information across a lot of different sites. Everywhere you share data it's recorded; it can be connected to you. Google yourself. Everyone should Google themselves every now and then to see what is out there about them.

Think about WHAT you're sharing. Why would you write, 'I'm by the pool wherever,' to let the world know that your home's empty. So there's that side of it as well. Just give it up, just go away and enjoy, and connect to life again without the digital technology. Believe it or not, that is possible, and it is usually more satisfying.

## ACCEPTABLE BEHAVIOUR

Our thresholds of acceptability are getting higher and higher. We have access to so much that is potentally disturbing and is unregulated. Just because there is lots of nudity out there, doesn't mean we need to join in. If someone asks you to send them a nude or sexy picture of yourself, or you feel the urge to for fun, think twice about how this picture could come back to haunt you. Do you really want your privacy invaded like that? It may not matter much to you right now, but what about in ten years' time? Think about it.

## SEARCHING FOR VALIDATION AND BELONGING

We all have this notion that we need to belong; we need to feel like we're wanted, that we fit in to the human race somehow, somewhere. If people are seeking that online, it's vital to be aware of the potential consequences. It may be that you don't get what you're looking for or you get more than you bargained for: it's very easy to be ignored or ridiculed online and that can have a huge impact on self-esteem. Be aware of the consequences of how you behave with others online too. Posting negative or unkind comments just to be funny can potentially hurt others as much as if you said it to their face. If you can't say anything nice then don't say anything at all.

Our obsessive 'like culture' is all about validation. It's easy to feel that if you get ten likes, that's ten affirmations and you are doing good – you are an acceptable human being. This also means that if you get lots of likes for saying or posting something negative or unkind you might feel that your behaviour is acceptable, when it isn't. Be aware that posting anything just to get likes can lead to self-destructive behaviour and damage others. Importantly, 'likes' online, often from strangers, can never create the happy hormones in the brain that are released from real human interaction.

One thing we can all do with the technology we have access to now is actually edit how we look and so present what we feel are improved (in some cases radically different) versions of our faces and our bodies. Though it can be fun to put an **'add ons' filter** on your images, it can become obsessive, so much so that without realizing it we are rejecting real selves for not being good enough. Think about how sad that is! What you look like in real life counts the most. Look in the mirror, pull fun faces at your real reflection – it's sometimes hard to remember what we look like if we're constantly viewing it through a screen with animated 'Disney character' eyes stuck on over our own.

Online dating can give us a sense of 'limitlessness' when it comes to potential partners, and creates a flippancy when it comes to meeting people. Awareness of both your behaviour and that of others is particularly important here. Be aware of weird behaviour, be cautious and manage your expectations. If you are searching for 'love' rather than 'fun', you need to be extra careful. Though online dating can be a decent and fun way to meet people, it's not the ONLY ANSWER. If you want to try it, you should research which one is the right one for you (there are SO many), you should ALWAYS meet someone in a public space and remember that people can be totally different to who they say they are online. Like I said earlier, the ability to edit words and pictures means people can misrepresent themselves to a ridiculous degree without thinking about what they're doing. An extreme example of this is catfishing.

*Catfishing is an online dating phenomenon where one person creates a fake identity to woo another, often using fake pictures and a fake name. Sometimes a lot of time is spent building a relationship via messaging and emails, but lots of it is based on lies. The longer it goes on, the more time and emotion you invest in that person, building up an image of them in your head that you really want to be true. Catfish relationships can go on for a long time, and typically don't result in a meet-up. But if the deceit is uncovered, the fall-out for the person who has been fooled can be very damaging. The catfish themselves isn't always a bad person. A lot of the time their own insecurities, their own low self-esteem, is why they don't want to come clean. This is why it's important that we should all be cautious, take care of ourselves and don't invest in someone you have never met.*

## DIGITAL DETOX

So, now you know all the pros and cons, it's time to shake up your internet life and possibly take a step back. That feeling of crappiness you have constantly looking at your phone? It might be down to over-use, to your loss of perspective.

Monitor the amount of time you spend online. Ask yourself honestly: *could* you be using some of your **time more productively?**

It can be fun to experiment by logging out of your social media accounts from time to time. Test how long you can survive, note if you feel any different. Another good way of trying this is to switch off notifications on your phone, or by taking off your email on mobile devices. It can help you feel **less frazzled. Read a book, plug in your iPod, go hiking, get your actual camera and go and take some beautiful pictures. Enjoy your Real Life.**

# IRL VS URL QUIZ, ANYONE?

**When you put your phone or device down after a boredom-filling sesh, you realize you've been looking at it for . . .**

**A** Between 0–30 minutes.

**B** Between 30 minutes to an hour.

**C** More than an hour.

**On holiday you and your phone . . .**

**A** Have a much needed break from each other and it is switched off most of the time.

**B** Comes everywhere with you, but you only check it a couple of times a day and make a point of not posting too much on social media.

**C** Are letting all your mates see constantly what amazoid food you are eating, how much you are in love with the sights, your sun-kissed body and perfected holiday pose.

**When you are online you are mostly . . .**

**A** On social media talking to your friends and looking at cute dogs.

**B** Doing a) above and ordering stuff you don't need.

**C** Doing all of a) and b) above and you sometimes end up down rabbit holes looking at stuff that makes you feel a bit icky.

**Which statement do you agree with the most on the subject of what's acceptable to share online (even in a private-message capacity)?**

**A** I would never post anything I wouldn't say out loud or would hate my family to see.

**B** I sometimes regret being a little ranty/over-excited.

**C** I definitely have shared images, messages or comments I regret.

**If someone's written something nasty about you online, do you . . .**

**A** Report them straight away?

**B** Feel upset, reply to them and then try to forget about it?

**C** Stew on it for a long time, thinking their nasty words might be true?

**How many tabs do you usually have open at one time when on the computer?**

**A** 1–5

**B** 5–10

**C** More

**Have you noticed how, when you search for something, similar products are advertised for you at a later date, sometimes on different sites?**

**A** Yes, you are aware that cookies store up to create your digital footprint and that advertisers work with this information so they know how to target you.

**B** You've noticed but you try not think about it too much.

**C** You had NO idea.

**With your best mate you would prefer to . . .**

**A** Go to the cinema.

**B** Skype – it's easier to fit in.

**C** You have loads of best mates and most of them you keep in touch with on endless WhatsApp chat.

99

### MOSTLY As - You're an IRLer, ella, ella!

You are mainly motivated by things in real life and feel you have a healthy under-standing and grip of how the online world can affect you. You protect yourself and harness your online time and relationships carefully. You mostly live your life in the real world and don't really understand how people take it all so seriously.

### MOSTLY Bs - You're the common keyboarder!

You are likely to end up stuck in an online hole for a little longer than you'd like sometimes, but you are keen to brush up on your knowledge of the ever-evolving technology.

Head to **www.bbc.co.uk/webwise** for guides and answers to lots of questions on internet facts and safety.

### MOSTLY Cs - You're a cybermaniac!

You are probably spending a little too much time online and sometimes feel a bit down, but don't know why. You act impulsively online and don't always think about what you are putting out there. It's time to try not to always rely on your phone and devices for company. Reconnect with the real world and challenge yourself. Don't have your mobile near when you are eating food with people. Read a book from cover to cover. Spend a whole Sunday with your phone switched off and no access to a computer or connected device. It would also be a good idea to head to the WebWise site suggested above in MOSTLY Bs so that you can get clued up on certain things about being online and, with the basics under your belt, still enjoy surfing the web.

# D-I-Y EXPRESSION

Immerse yourself in the good stuff: stuff that makes you happy, that helps you create and celebrate your world the way you want to. One of the ways of doing this is to start your own zine – a collection of stories, ideas, visuals and writing on the types of subjects you are interested in and that you think the world might be lacking.

101

# GAL POWER

gal-dem.com is a creative online magazine comprising the contributions of over seventy women of colour. They wanted people of different shapes, sizes, genders and ethnic backgrounds to engage with the work they are doing. They published their first print edition in September 2016.

gal-dem editor Liv has provided *Open Your Mind* with five tips on how to start a zine.

**1** One of the first things we decided on for the magazine was the theme. Deciding on a clear theme made deciding the rest somewhat straightforward. We knew what sort of pieces we wanted and which writers, artists and photographers would be a good fit. In terms of producing a coherent magazine, this was key!

**2** The second key point is being clear with the sort of pieces you want to publish. We put out an open call for submissions, but we didn't accept every single idea. It can be really tricky deciding what content to publish, but it largely came down to us not wanting to reproduce similar pieces and maintain our chatty gal-dem tone. There will always be pieces which simply don't fit! I know when I first started editing I hated having these conversations – but there are definitely ways to be diplomatic.

**3** Reaching out to people whose work you *fan-girl* over. Many of the photographers and writers involved in this print were people whose work I loved and hadn't worked with before. Our budget was non-existent (and print is very expensive!), so we had to reach out to people and be open and honest about what it was we could offer, but mainly getting them on board with the ethos behind gal-dem. If you are backing a worthy cause, the chances are people will rally behind you if they can.

**4** You will always find the odd mistake in print, particularly if it's your first one. But the best way to minimize risk is to have a rigorous team of editors and sub-editors. All pieces should be looked at a minimum of twice. It's definitely best not to leave this until the eleventh hour, when you are tired and have been staring at the same pages for hours. Get different people to check different pieces as they will always find something you may miss.

**5** Print is expensive and there will always be hidden costs. So the final tip would have to be always overestimate how much things will cost, and set up things like pre-orders beforehand. Fortunately I had friends and family who offered to lend me money without asking, but we still ended up going over budget. We ordered as many copies as we could to keep our costs down and it definitely paid off. People are willing to pay for something substantial – they generally want something which they can pop on their coffee table and flick through at their own leisure.

Head to www.gal-dem.com for more.

# THAT'S WHAT SHE SAID

There are so many exciting grassroots movements out there, one of them being *thatswhatss*, an amazing photography and expression platform for girls. I spoke to **Izzy Whiteley** from That's What She Said – thatswhatss – about what drives her.

**GC:** **What is thatswhatss, exactly?**

**I:** That's What She Said is a photography-based project that aims to be the middleman between young girls and non-binary teens and society. We go around the UK, working on creative projects, with the aim of creating an open line of communication between these young people and society. It is ultimately about giving them a voice - away from the judgement of peers, teachers and parents. The topics are about everything relating to girlhood.

I really want to give girls and non-binary teens a platform to voice their opinions. I want to encourage them to question society and make a project that will force the issue, because we are bringing up a generation of girls that don't believe in themselves and, more importantly, are silenced. Many of them don't even know they have opinions until you ask them a certain question and it all comes pouring out.

We also have a 'She Said' section for submissions, which can be anything from art, essays, random thoughts and poems, to videos and music. From these submissions I find creative ways to write their quotes and share them on Instagram. All we want is to capture the beauty of reality, and give these teens space and safety to talk about issues that they often feel people don't care about or don't think are important. It is giving the power back to people and, hopefully, encouraging them to fight for change.

**GC:** **Why did you feel the need to create it?**

**I:** When I was a young girl, I never really questioned why I felt so bad. I felt ugly, fat, inadequate – not good enough for society and men. From what I read in magazines and in the media and through talking to friends, I felt that it was normal to be a girl and feel bad. Everything around me was telling me that I was flawed and that I needed to be better. We expect girls to feel ugly, cry all the time, be weak and take dangerous measures to change their appearance because 'it's just what girls do'. We did not come out of the vagina hating our thighs and sexualizing ourselves. This is what we have been taught.

When creating thatswhatss I felt like we never hear real experiences — just facts, figures and percentages. Though data collection is sometimes the only way, there is so much more info and things to learn from each teen's voice — and, more importantly, they are the ones that can tell us what to change. I wanted to listen to their experiences, pain, worries, fears, find out what they need, and take it to where it needs to go.

I realized quickly that teens need to be educated about this idea of conditioning and the blame that is put on us surrounding 'choice'. Choice is not simply black and white — it is shades of grey, which represent the pressures that make us choose to do, or not do, something. Some of these choices we are aware of, and some we aren't. All these particular choices such as dieting, changing our appearance, sexualization, etc. are being made in a society where women are still not economically, politically or socially equal. From the day a girl is born, she is bombarded with more and more signs that her worth is in her looks. Feminism is just much more complicated now as the issues aren't so black and white; many issues are subtle and harder to understand. There can be this ugly 'uncool' stigma around feminism, which makes teens not want to be part of it — thatswhatss represents the individual's voice and that's why I chose to start it.

It takes a lot of confidence and self-assurance to be an activist — thatswhatss is a space where young girls and non-binary teens can talk about these issues without having to fight against everyone. There are so many extremes of feminism, which when you are just starting out can be really intimidating. I wanted to give teens a way to just dip their foot in and start understanding the injustice.

**GC:** Do you have any tips for those out there who want to create something similar?

**I:** Research the hell out of it. See what's out there. See how your idea is different. It's good when it comes from your own experiences, because the passion always comes through. Make sure you have support and people who believe in you, who can help you along the way. You don't have to have everything figured out before you start; you can change and grow as you go along. Contact and reach out to everyone and anyone, but don't be disheartened when people don't reply, even after the fifth email. I have contacted and chased so, so much press. Rejection can be hard to deal with, but people are so busy, and you are often asking for help without offering anything. Don't take it personally.

Ask advice and learn from people. I have had so many meetings with people that I thought would be 'the big break', and they have turned into nothing — which is OK, because you keep learning, but it can be a bit annoying. Make sure it is something you really enjoy, because you will be spending a lot of your free time on it.

Head to www.thatswhatss.com for more info.

Instagram @thatswhatss

107

# VOLUNTEERING

Is something so fabulous to do!

Fabulous for your mind, fabulous for skill building, fabulous for the organization you offer your time to, fabulous for your community. Volunteering can take up as little or as much of your life as you want it to. There are an abundance of schemes offering the opportunity to get involved in a way that suits you.

For example, you could go on the Age UK website, sign up and before you know it you could end up making a new friend in someone older and wiser who can offer you a different perspective on life. Volunteering to work in Oxfam shops would be a fantastic way to gain shop-floor skills and meet new people. Plus specialist organizations can even arrange volunteering opportunities for you abroad.

108

# THE SCARY WORLD

Your world is often what you make it . . . but some people
feel like they have had that choice taken away from them,
and like they want to run away. Do you ever feel like that?
Are you worried about someone who does?

109

Running away can mean putting yourself in a very unsafe situation – and will change the lives of those you are running away from too. It's an extremely serious thing to do. Both parties need to know that there is help out there.

I spoke to the amazing fire-flame that is Karen Robinson from Missing People about the incredible organization. She tells us:

Running away is not always necessarily a deliberate thing. A lot of people find themselves in a situation where they need to get out and they go — they don't make a decision necessarily to vanish from their life, but once they're gone it's sometimes very hard to come back.

A lot of missing adults who've been found safe and well and who've returned talk about a series of small decisions, find it gets harder and harder to contact whatever 'home' is. So they end up being missing because they might think to themselves, 'Well, how do I explain? If I didn't go home tonight, how would I explain to my boyfriend tomorrow why I didn't go home tonight?' So then it becomes, 'Well, I'll stay away another night.' And then, 'How do I explain why I was away for two nights? By that time, my whole family will know. How am I going to explain to my family what's going on in my head?'

So it's more complicated than you see in films. We know that around 250,000 people a year will go missing, and two-thirds of those are under eighteen — they're children — but that's just the ones that we know about.

If you are a missing person, I think the most important thing is to get help from someone you trust. You might not want to re-approach your life, and that's completely OK. It's OK not to want to be in touch with the people who are missing you. It's perfectly OK; it's not a crime. The charity Missing People is not going to judge you for that and we are here twenty-four hours a day, confidentially and for free. Anyone can call or text us on the number 116000 day or night and we will listen and help. We will never judge you.

So we would encourage people to contact us if they want some completely anonymous, confidential, neutral support, or a space to think through their options. We will help the person decide what they want, what to do next and help them be connected to a safe place or adult. Sometimes we make three-way calls to social workers and police, or we help people access help from a local hostel so they can have a warm bed for the night. We never rush people. It can take time to work out how you feel and decide what you want and that's OK.

We can pass a message home if someone wants to send their family or carers a message if they aren't ready to speak to them yet. It's sometimes the first step. Through our helpline, we speak to tens of thousands of people every year who do want to let their loved ones know that they're OK, but aren't ready to go back. We'll pass messages between them — and/or pass a message home . . . until they're ready to be in touch. There are so many emotions in there, but we can be a bit of a bridge between the two.

If the situation you are running from is unsafe, you don't have to go back. You don't have to love where you are living, and you don't have to love someone just because they're your blood relative. It's OK to be angry with your relatives or your carers (if you're living in care). We can reconnect people via three-way calls as well — not necessarily with their loved ones; quite often it will be with the police, or a social worker, or a teacher — somebody who is a safe adult.

Trust your gut — if you're worried about someone, it's probably for a good reason. If you can't find them and it's out of the ordinary and you're concerned, ring the police and report them missing. The police will ask you lots of questions and decide if and how they can help. Try to reach the person yourself, contact other people they hang out with and try to work out what's going on. Then contact us at the charity Missing People by calling or texting 116000. We can help you clear your head a bit, and go, 'Right, have you thought of this? Are there other children in the house?' If it's a missing child, people literally go into shock, panic, trauma mode. We are here to help you, guide you and support you at what will be one of the most frightening moments of your life.

Most missing people will be found very quickly, and they'll be found safe and well. More than ninety per cent of people will be found within twenty-four hours. A tiny fraction of people who go missing will stay missing for a long period of time, and some of them stay missing for years or even decades. Missing People will be with that family throughout, and hold their hand through it all.

Go to **www.missingpeople.org.uk** for more information on this brilliant charity and how it can help.

# PREJUDICE

**Noun**: *a preconceived optinion that is not based on reason or actual experience*

## HATE IS A WASTE – RACISM A DISGRACE

Us humans have complicated and active brains pulling us in many directions. We are full of contradictions; at times we cavort like a rhino on champagne, but then – within the blink of an eye – revert to a terrified mouse. Our morality is easily twisted, our hopes and dreams yanked in one direction and then the other as we bumble through life, the temptations of greed, and sour grapes of envy and discontent sometimes blurring our once-clear vision.

Humans like order, routine, things going as planned, a box to tick. It helps us feel like we have everything under control. Unfortunately for some, we live in a world that is a hotbed of change, a feast of opinions and stories to tell, and it can make us uneasy and fearful – and sometimes this oozes out of us in a toxic thing called PREJUDICE. And it's the ugliest of ugly when it does.

Hate is a waste; racism a disgrace – and to be influenced by prejudice is cutting yourself off from a world of discovery. We are all flesh and bone, trying to work our way through life – so let's do it together, as one. It will make it all so much less lonely.

If you hear someone voicing hatred or prejudice, even if they are someone close to you, gently challenge why they feel strongly enough to spout negativity. If you experience or witness a hate crime of any sort – this includes physical and/or verbal abuse – it is very important that it is reported to the police.

113

We should all know that racist behaviour is unacceptable. But, while some of us know full well what racism is, others may not realize exactly what defines racism. Here are some things to look out for and guard against doing:

## Things that are racist/offensive

Touching people's hair because it's culturally different to yours. I spent a lot of my youth with girls yanking gently and lovingly at my braid extensions. It didn't really anger me or anything; it's nice for people to show an interest. But grabbing people's hair is quite an invasion of space, and kinda makes that person feel a little like a clown!

Assuming someone will act a certain way or do certain things or have a certain mindset because of their religion or the colour of skin. You don't know anyone till you know them – so ask questions to find out what they're about rather than making assumptions.

Using inflammatory racist names. It doesn't matter if you hear other people using them – never use these words.

The following suggestions are provided by twenty-four-year-old Hanna Yusuf:

Casually dropping in comments about the headscarf being a symbol of oppression. I get that in some countries that have oppressive regimes women wear the headscarf, but in liberal countries throughout Europe the headscarf is a part of people's identity. To casually say that it's a symbol of oppression is not just wrong; it's also hugely offensive. How would you like it if something that's part of your identity and that you feel comfortable wearing was labelled as an endorsement of something abhorrent?

114

Conflating cultural practices with the religion of Islam. Female genital mutilation (FGM) and honour killings are not prescribed by Islam. Some people that carry out those horrible practices happen to be Muslim, but the practitioners aren't exclusively Muslim. It's highly offensive when people don't take the time to learn the facts before making these wrong claims.

Assuming that I'm married or asking about my marital status, as if that is relevant. I don't need a husband to live my life, thank you very much. (This applies to all women of all religions, to be honest.)

# Things that aren't racist/offensive

Using the correct term for someone's cultural identity as a way of describing someone in a non-derogatory way, for example, 'She was the tall white girl with ginger hair at the party.'

Asking someone when appropriate and in an inquisitive and kind way about their culture or heritage.

Supporting anti-racial campaigns regardless of your own skin colour or background. In the same way that a man can be a feminist, you don't have to be repressed or attacked yourself to back anti-racism movements.

# FEMINISM

IT'S EASY:
YOU ARE A
FEMINIST
IF YOU BELIEVE
IN EQUALITY FOR
MEN AND
WOMEN.

116

A lot of people think it's a little grumpy, but feminism is pretty awesome. It's essentially a powerful belief that we live in a patriarchal society (a society essentially run and governed by men) and that this ain't cool. To be a feminist in the most basic of terms means to believe in equality. Some feminists campaign for it societally, domestically and professionally in a number of ways. Feminists believe that the objectification of women, which has very much been ingrained in us, is damaging, disturbing and undermining. Feminists do not believe that men are evil or that women are better than men. They believe that women are equally as valuable and important in society as men and should be treated as such, and not be valued or judged by their looks – or feel that they have to dress any particular way – or judged by their ability to reproduce, but by their equal contribution to the workplace and beyond. Feminism makes sense. Calling yourself a feminist does not tag you as a man-hater or someone who does not like to be feminine – it tags you as someone who believes in equality. Women can be beautiful and powerful, they can be leaders and carers, they can be loud and wild if they choose or just one or none of those things if they choose. Women are almightily dynamic. Being a feminist means you are a champion of the rights of other women to achieve all that they are capable of. Many men are feminists too.

There is a fascinating and rich tapestry of feminist movements out there, not one size fits all. We all have different reference points and experiences. There so many sections of feminism for this reason. Research them for yourself and enjoy finding out which thread of activism/campaign/literature works for you. Once you start to look, there will be thousands of entry points to a wonderful and fulfilling feminism that appeals to you. I warn you, though, it can be overwhelming. Don't exhaust yourself thinking you are the only warrior having to think about it all, all the time. There isn't enough time in a lifetime to right all the wrongs. Feminism isn't about one person being the saviour, it's about respect and togetherness and fairness. Don't forget to have some fun too.

**So, are you a feminist?**

YES ☐   NO ☐

If yes, then welcome aboard.

## FURTHER READING ON FEMINISM

*Girl Up* by Laura Bates

*How to Be a Woman* by Caitlin Moran

*What's a Girl Gotta Do?* by Holly Bourne

*What is Feminism? Why Do We Need It? And Other Big Questions* by Bea Appleby and Louise Spilsbury

*Bad Feminist* by Roxane Gay

*My Life on the Road* by Gloria Steinem

*We Should All Be Feminists* by Chimamanda Ngozi Adichie

117

# TRAVEL

STOCKHOLM

BERLIN

LONDON

PARIS

NEW YORK
TORONTO

ISTANBUL

ATHENS

MARRAKESH

MEXICO CITY

RIO

CAPE TOWN

Where do you want to go? Look at the map of the world . . .
the BIG, beautiful world. Now it's time to dream wildly and
think big about other cultures, other landscapes, how the rest of
the world lives. Mark the places you'd love to see . . . Let your
imagination guide you.

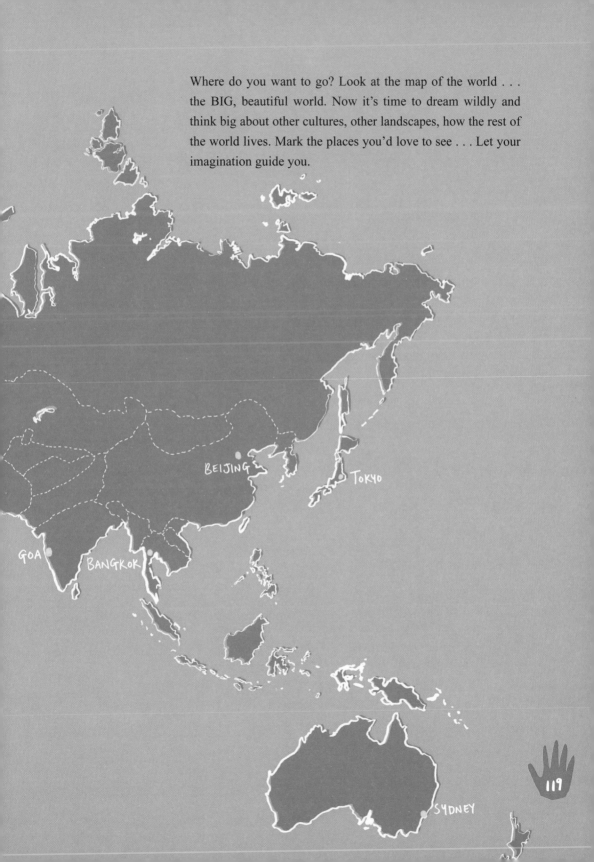

BEIJING

TOKYO

GOA

BANGKOK

SYDNEY

119

# FINDING WHERE YOU BELONG

Travel can mean a permanent move to somewhere. Sometimes your dreams belong in another country. I spoke to **Lucy**, who made the decision at age twenty-two to leave the UK and move to Greece. Lucy thinks she would never have been able to have the quality of life and the happiness she has now if she had stayed in the UK.

I'm Lucy and I'm from Southampton, but I live in Greece with my husband and young son where I co-manage our family's four-star hotel.

When I was twenty-two years old, a mixture of unhappy events, struggling with London life and poor health led me to decide that I needed to make a change in my life. Leaving my family and friends (my second family) was really hard, but I knew it was the right thing for me to do.

My lifestyle is different in every way to what I had imagined when I was growing up: different career, different culture and different people around me in my everyday life. Working in a hotel rather than on the stage was not what I had envisaged when I was practising accepting my Olivier award in the mirror as a twelve-year-old. But other things came into my life that I hadn't realized, expected (or maybe accepted?) would be so important to me. It took me a long time to interpret that as success rather than failure. Learning to grab change (in all its forms) by the balls is probably the key to most of my achievements.

# WANDERLUST + EXPRESSION

121

# A STRONG DESIRE TO TRAVEL

I have a rampant sense of wanderlust within me. I am addicted to far-flung places and new worlds within my world. It makes my eyes feel like they could pop out of my head with glee and happiness when I travel. The first day of this year, I woke up on the fringes of the jungle in Costa Rica. Through the netting in the wooden hut we were staying in, I could see the black curly tail of a monkey. Later that day, I spotted a lime-green beaked toucan, many, many feet above me on the top of the trees.

I would never have believed back at the start of my career – which I love and have worked hard at for eight years – that I would one day be in a position to travel so widely. I would never have thought I'd trek Mount Kenya for charity and cycle to Paris in my lifetime. I never knew I would be happy enough with my own company to fly long-haul or eat dinner in restaurants alone – or have the courage to go to Sierra Leone in West Africa after a severe outbreak during the Ebola epidemic.

I spent my teenage years preparing for a life that didn't factor in time for adventure – I'm not sure why. I guess, despite having access to a decent education, I didn't feel that sense of privilege that would allow me to dream of travel. I never felt worthy of some of life's spectacular experiences. I did grow up in a house with a mother who was open to the world. Having gone to an international school herself, my mum learned French at the age of fourteen to communicate with a boy she'd fallen in love with whilst living in Geneva, Switzerland. She then went on to high school in New York City till she was seventeen, after which she moved to Paris, where she lived on a mattress on the floor, and was a nanny to make ends meet. When I was a young child, Mum had friends from different backgrounds, with different strengths, flavours and stories to offer a small and always inquisitive little me.

But Mum's life has had twists and turns. She suffered trauma and mental-health battles too, and by the time I was teenager, that, along with my own monstrous experiences, had turned the fun into a struggle. And so, when I left home aged eighteen, I was a young person with a conflicted tangle of expectations for my own life. I'd grown up with the tools of expressive communication, and a soul fuelled by energy for experience, and yet I subconsciously prepared for life to be tough.

It wasn't just what I'd seen at home, either. I was in a world where women have to fight harder to gain the confidence to say what they want, to feel like they can be brave enough for ferocious adventure. In a world where it is rare to see darker skin tones than all shades of white represented as 'explorers' of the globe, I am immensely proud and thankful to have done the things I've done so far. To love the world as I do, and be able to take the plunge to go out and discover it . . . it feels like a gift to myself – one that I couldn't recommend more.

So, go to places; ignite your wanderlust! You don't need to go far – organize camping trips with friends, look upwards at the sky and enjoy the magic of clouds, play in the park and roll down hills always. Keep your imagination active; it'll protect you in the most confusing times. And, if you imagine and work hard enough, sometimes some of those dreams will come true. Love the real world and all it has to offer. The amount there is out there to experience and learn from is endless.

123

# MAKE RAINBOWS...

Anyone who knows me knows I am in love with colour. I strongly believe in its power to cheer and heal.

So much so that, a few years ago in London, I conducted a social experiment for a brand to brighten people's day.

My task was simply to spark the imaginations of those in the city, any way I saw fit. So between 6 a.m. and 10 a.m. on a Monday morning, I literally turned London Bridge into a rainbow. I specifically chose that day and those hours when life can be particularly challenging, when the relentless morning commute is enough to smash good vibes to smithereens, to make the happiest of people feel like they're having the colour bashed out of them.

The longest rainbow carpet I'll ever see in my life was rolled out across London Bridge, me situated at one end, in a matching rainbow jacket, giving passers-by a single flower each as they walked to work through a jaunty arch that said LOVE MONDAYS.

I'm sounding like a madwoman now, right? Here's the picture to prove it. I find myself again and again having to look at the pictures to believe it too.

What I found was that, although some people were suspicious, ninety per cent of faces broke into a smile . . . and it felt euphoric. A collective euphoria via colour! I watched anyone with their head down walk the full bridge and become dazzled by the rainbow beneath them. I will never forget that day. I got so many hugs. I noticed most people wore hues of brown, black and grey, their sartorial aesthetic blurring into the miserable weather around them.

As the opportunity to roll carpets as big as the BFG's feet is rare, think of alternative ways you can introduce colour and sparkle into your life. You can wear all the colours of the Northern Lights on your body. You can shimmer in sequins that shine as much as the sea on holiday. Fill your bedroom with vases of fire-coloured dahlias to make you smile. There is much power in the brightness of flowers.

AND DANCE. NEVER FORGET TO TURN MUSIC UP LOUD AND BOOGIE.

What would you do to spark your city/town/village community? Write/draw it below.

DO YOU KNOW WHAT YOU WANT TO BE WHEN YOU GROW UP?

I ASK YOU THIS, REGARDLESS OF YOUR AGE . . .

Allow me to let you into a little secret: hardly anyone knows for sure. Also, this whole 'growing up' thing is a bit of a myth. We may stop physically growing 'up', but we are always adding layers of experience, twisting and turning about the place, forming opinions, fusing, changing and emotionally growing.

So release yourself from the pressure of an 'algorithmic' ideal. Not everything happens in an efficient, prescribed sequence. Success isn't pinned on one exam paper, or on one interview . . . There isn't ONE straight route to anywhere or anything. The paths we must take are complicated, more like those of a maze, with choices to make in every direction and the occasional dead end – so don't be upset with yourself if you're unsure about where you're going, or exactly what will make you happiest. Just follow your instincts, use your imagination, use your brain and use every resource at your disposal.

TRY things. Lots of things. Meet people you admire and aspire to be like for tea. Talk about your maddest of madcap ideas. Collaborate with your peers – whether it's organizing a fundraising event, or setting up a blog. Exchanging thoughts and ideas – even if it's just to make each other laugh, and laugh, and laugh – is stimulating. It will get you thinking. Sparks will fly. You don't have to project too far ahead or rush headlong into your newfound goal or ideal . . . Savour every moment of learning; relish every challenge.

I want to pierce through the belief that success at school, or not messing up an internship, is the be-all and end-all. Everybody makes mistakes – think of them of as experiences, and learn from them. Do your best; try to be kind; work hard and relax. Weirdly, when you are relaxed you are usually the most confident – you are expressive and true, and therefore you will do your best. If you don't get the grade you wanted, or you don't get that job, you're not going to die. There will be a way, an alternative – and everything is going to be OK. So don't believe the hype that everything rests on one thing going right.

# Mentors & ✳ ✳ Role Models

**Role model**: *a person looked up to by others as an example to follow.*

Role models and mentors are invaluable. You are never too young or too old to have one. Of the things I'm most humbly grateful for in my life, all the generous-spirited people I have learned from are right up there at the top – whether it's those I call friends or those that I've taken the time to seek out, listen to and study. It's rewarding and important to spend time on researching incredible people of the past and present who embody a healthy and compassionate philosophy, message or energy that you can connect to in some way. It doesn't mean you should necessarily aspire to become them exactly – but educating yourself about aspirational figures is good for you.

Grace Jones

Erykah Badu

Spice Girls

The Slits

128

We are lucky to live in a time when we have access and exposure to a wealth of arts, cultures and subcultures so diverse they are a firework of fun to learn about and become inspired by. There are some incredible women, for example, who have offered sparks of irreverence that have inspired me over the years, and been awesome in helping me feel like it's OK to be me.

Who do you see that makes you feel excited to be you? Fill in the blanks with your own role-model firework.

129

**Mentor**: *an experienced and trusted adviser.*

A mentor in your life can enhance it greatly. There is a brilliant list of organizations at the back of the book that offer mentorship schemes of different types.

I mentor brilliant **June Eric-Udorie**. She is a writer and so impressively clever. She is eight years younger than me. We meet for a hot chocolate every few months and talk about what we're up to. For me, mentoring June has shown me how hard it is to be young right now, and how so many young people are inspiringly unselfish – they are, in fact, supremely advanced thinkers who want a better society for all. They are less reckless than I was at that age, more thoughtful. I want to let June know just how awesome she is. In return, she gave me some amazing advice when I first told her about this book. She sent me many awesome reading lists and pieces written by the best writers on the subject of writing. June knows SO much, and I learn from her every time we hang out.

**GC:** **What do you get out of having a mentor?**

**JE-U:** There are lots of benefits to having a mentor — someone who can guide you with decisions [about] your career or just life in general . . . They provide insight, push you to think differently, and help remind you of your value and worth. But I think the best thing about having [Gem] as a mentor is just being able to learn from her. I watch as my mentor takes up space and is brave and fun and jolly and smart, and the ways in which she practises the lessons that she's trying to teach me. It's heart-warming, knowing there's someone you can always reach out to, but it's even better having a mentor that embodies the sort of person you want to be. You can look up to her when you're not feeling as motivated or courageous. I find myself thinking, 'What would Gemma do?'

**GC:** **Do you mentor anyone?**

**JE-U:** I do a little bit of academic mentoring with Integrate, a Bristol-based charity that works primarily with black, minority, ethnic and refugee kids in the UK. I really enjoy it, but in the future I'd really like to mentor black girls and young women, because I think it's so important that they have cheerleaders and supporters and people who are on their side, especially when we live in a world where we are still, very much, relegated to the shadows.

My mentor is a badass of a woman called Karen Blackett. She's witty, smart and graciously brave, and is the CEO of one of the UK's most influential media companies. Karen advises on and creates content for some of the UK's biggest advertising campaigns. She also has a fabulous glass office, with lovely photographs everywhere, and everyone around her respects her immensely.

131

## Talking to Karen Blackett, OBE

**GC:**
**KB:**

**What do you get out of being a mentor?**

By mentoring someone else, it actually leads to reverse-mentoring. I get to draw on my experience to help someone else, but I also learn and challenge my brain. The gift of helping others is a blessing. Seeing someone else progress and achieve is a massive reward. I genuinely believe with the right support and guidance, determination and resilience, work ethic and focus, anyone can achieve their goals. We have it within us to make our dreams, however big or small, a reality.

**GC:**
**KB:**

**Who is your mentor?**

Lawyer, businesswoman and broadcaster Dame Heather Rabbatts.

## Talking to Dame Heather Rabbatts

**GC:**
**DHR:**

**What do you get out of being a mentor?**

I think what I get out of being a mentor is always learning. Mentoring is two-way . . . in trying to offer insight to others, you inevitably reflect on your own experiences and different perspectives evolve. I totally value the development for both the mentee and myself, and know it enriches my life.

I have never had a mentor as such but for me my group of women friends have always been there and offered great guidance and support — so I have been truly blessed!

132

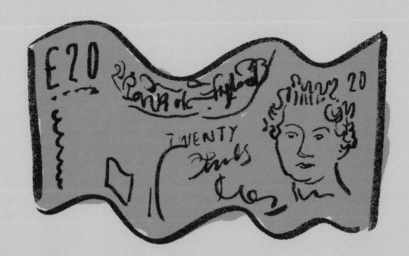

# MONEY MONEY MONEY

133

# ...AKA: CASHOLA, SPONDULAS, WONGA, NOTES, DOLLAR DOLLAR BILL, Y'ALL.

*I have expensive ta$te*

Money = a scramble. Either a scramble to get it, or a scramble to use it wisely if you have some. We all need money to live, and it's great to have a bit extra – to go out, go on holidays, buy nice things. But money can mess you up too. If you don't have enough, it is miserable: it can lead to health problems; it's tough on friendships; it can make you despair. If you have too much, it can set you apart from friends; it doesn't make you a better person; it doesn't stop you feeling lonely . . . It doesn't solve your problems.

Life is like a game of Monopoly, involving luck, decisions and moral choices. Whatever your money situation – the main thing is to be in control of your finances. Don't let money control you – don't become obsessed with it. Do develop healthy attitudes to money early on. Learn to live within your means. Clue yourself up about saving and what different kinds of bank accounts entail and mean for you. We don't get taught about the practicalities of money at school, which is bizarre, as it is so pivotal to security and stability – even our health. So it's up to YOU to get smart.

134

I spoke to an awesome charity called My Bnk, which believes money should be a subject on the curriculum. My Bnk visits schools, colleges and universities to explain some of the hard-to-understand basics.

Drink it up: some of these words could save ya some money.

As a nation, we can be obsessed with money. For different reasons, though. For some, it comes from a place of goodwill — they are obsessed with the bigger picture, like setting up their own business and striving to make a success of it. Some let money govern them unhealthily; others think about it a lot, and it affects their emotional well-being because they don't have enough. Our attitude to credit is changing. Older generations were much more credit-loving, which led to a lot of people in deep debt. That's changing, and we're collectively getting more savvy to how that can go wrong.

# MONEY

## KEY TERMS AND TOP TIPS

The key things to remember are **simple**, really.

**Credit is borrowed money.** When you have a credit card, you are borrowing money, which, if you don't pay it back within a certain time period, you are charged interest on. This interest is different depending on who you borrow the money from. But essentially it means you're going to have to pay back more than you borrowed in the first place. Credit cards aren't bad things if you use them wisely; they can help with emergencies, for example. As long as you know that it isn't your money and that you must pay it back as soon as possible.

When considering a credit card for the first time, it's important to not get reeled in by the 'glamour' aspect of 'plastic'. It can feel so much better to pay for things with your own hard-earned cash.

**Payday lenders.** There are lots of different angles to these, but, essentially, they work on a similar premise to credit. They make money by charging high interest rates on the cash they lend you.

**Debt** is money you owe.

**Incorporating an income timeline.** It's never too early think about an income timeline. Making sure your income and outgoings line up now will help when you are managing your finances as an adult. If you have learned **budgeting** and **saving** skills before you're eighteen, then you're less likely to need to borrow money – and, if you *do* borrow it, you're going to understand why you're borrowing it, and it'll be structured.

136

**Inform yourself as a consumer.** Where's your money going? Know that you've essentially got control.

**Types of accounts.** There are enough to bamboozle even the smartest of folk out there. Remember this and do your research. There are **current accounts** and **savings accounts** – that's as complicated as it should really get. But they're all called different things: a **flex account**, a **gold account**, a **platinum account** – they've all got different names according to different banks. **Compare the AER (annual equivalent rate)** on accounts if you want to be a **saver**. If you're looking at **borrowing** , then you need to **compare the APR (annual percentage rate)**. It's so refreshing to have the tools to find what you want in a bank account. So look up the small print and ask questions when you're in the bank.

**Overdrafts.** These are super common because they're seen as a 'safety net'. Often people start with them at university, when they're interest free. They are helpful if you need a little extra money at the end of the month; but, as with other forms of credit, they do need to be paid back.

**University.** At the moment, a three-year university course will cost around **£50,000**, which covers **tuition fees** and a **maintenance loan**. It's important not to focus too heavily on the 'owing' and think about the benefits of **learning and experience** that you get from university, as it's all too easy to become overwhelmed. If you do decide to go, remember that it's important to plan in advance how you are going to **budget** your money whilst there. Also remember that you don't have to start paying these loans back until you're earning over a certain salary threshold after you have graduated.

If you have a **dream**, be **passionate** and **source** the right help. There are loads of **cool organizations** out there that **support young people's businesses** – that will help you get **grants** and get **funding**. You just have to have a **good idea**, engage a **strong sense of identity** and **focus**. Be **confident**, **positive**, know your market, do your **research**. Ask yourself – **has anything been done like this before?** Have you tried and **tested it** – or has someone else tested it, and it flopped? Why did it flop? Learn from their mistakes and be patient.

**Tax.** Don't forget it. You'll pay income tax on income above your Personal Allowance.

Know your tax status, and how you're paying yours – whether you are saving it each month if you're self-employed, or if it is deducted at source by your employer.

## DON'T PANIC!

### THERE ARE LOTS OF PEOPLE
### YOU CAN ASK FOR ADVICE . . .

Great money-management apps are:

**Toshl Finance** – a spending app that helps track your outgoings.

**OnTrees** – all your bank accounts on one platform.

**ClearScore** – free credit score and report on your phone.

138

# BUDGET PLANNER

## INCOME

Saturday or part-time job

Parental allowance

(Occasionally selling stuff on eBay)

## OUTGOINGS

Clothes/sports stuff

Beauty products

Phone bill

Music/TV/games downloads/books or DVDs

Hobbies

Cinema

Meals out

Snacks/drinks

Tampons and other life essentials

## OCCASIONAL COSTS

Birthday or Christmas gifts

Long-distance travel

Holidays

Gigs/festivals/events

Hair – cut or colour

Nail bar/other beauty treatments

Gadgets/computer

# CAREERS

I believe you can be anything you want to be in this world. Anyone can be. I truly believe it. You don't have to be what your mum or dad wishes, what a 'career advisor' advises or even what you thought you might be at a different point in your life. The clichés are true: if you work hard enough, your dreams can come true. I believe that because mine did, and more. Your dreams change, too, as you grow. That's part of the fun.

## The hula hooper

What you personally want to be in life might jump outside convention and bend others' minds. I interviewed one such irreverent, imaginative, gutsy, hard-grafting woman: the global bend machine that is *Marawa The Amazing*. Marawa is a world-record-holding professional hula hooper and is toppest of top in the hula hooping game.

**GC:** How does one end up being a professional hula hooper? Is it something that you always wanted to do?

**M:** No, not at all . . . I think it could've easily been something else. I really didn't know, going into it, what I was doing. The key thing was that I studied a Bachelor of Circus Arts degree, and ended up getting into the circus. It was a brand-new degree, and I thought that it sounded really interesting. I didn't know where it was going to lead; I didn't know it was going to lead to being a professional hula hooper! I did gymnastics in high school. I really liked arty stuff, but was encouraged to follow an academic route, and I did two years of social science and creative writing at university. I really liked sociology, and I really liked writing, but I wasn't convinced that it was the course for me, and I didn't know what I would do for a job at the end of it.

Then in my early/mid-twenties I got into the circus school, and I was like, 'Right then, let's give this a go!' And ever since then I've felt like I was not *getting away with it*, but I felt like I was on holiday all the time. I was turning up in a tracksuit every day, and my job was to climb up some ropes and work on my flexibility, which felt like the best thing ever. It felt like a holiday. Then getting into shows, and doing shows, I was like, 'This is not work. This is the best fun ever — literally.'

**GC:** How did you translate going to circus school into a career and business and being able to travel the world?

**M:** I was really lucky. I get paid enough that I can do the things I want to do and save a bit too. And I've chosen a skill that I can keep doing until I'm seventy-five.

141

**GC:** Tell me about the troupe.

**M:** That was a project with the Roundhouse where they asked me to choreograph a group to do a group hoop performance for the Olympic torch relay. We did the project and it worked really well. We had twelve girls, and I taught them. Some of them weren't hoopers at all — they just wanted to be in it. So we taught them how to hoop, and put the routine together . . . Now I can step back a little bit and train up the next generation of hoopers.

**GC:** What does your family think of your job?

**M:** I'd managed to get away with not telling my dad until I was thirty. He thought I'd finished my social science degree, and then he wasn't really sure what I was doing. He likes to Skype with me every now and then just to remind me that I might want to come home and finish my studies and get serious again.

**GC:** What are your top tips about travel?

**M:** Shelter, food, safety. That's it. Book your flight, book a cheap hostel — do your research, find a reputable place to stay. You can go anywhere in the world. Just leave the hotel and just walk. I'll just walk and walk and walk, and try and keep it relatively simple so you don't need a map. That's how I think you really get a taste for a place.

## The comedian

How amazing is it to have a career out of making people laugh? Being a comedian is an ACTUAL job. I talked to the awesome, smart and funny *Aisling Bea* about how to get into the world of 'comedy'.

# Aisling's advice

Start in your sitting room entertaining your cat, and upgrade to your friends, then strangers. Practise speaking your bits out loud. Record yourself, on paper and on your phone. Start bringing a notebook with you everywhere and jot down things that happen. For stand-up, get stage time, hop on everywhere, start your own gigs if there are none, hone your craft, throw yourself into it and make a community of fellow artists so you can all help bring each other up. Talk to everyone. Don't ask everyone for their opinion, only people you trust. And TRY and enjoy it — you are aiming to make people a bit happier. Stay focused on that. Wear shoes you feel make you confident so you can plant your feet properly. YOU GOT THIS.

It is not hard to get into comedy — what is tough is STAYING in comedy. When you have a bad gig, or someone is mean, or you feel that cringe of silence and don't want to ever see people again, or when you don't make money and have to trek around and sleep on couches, or if you get writer's block, that is hard. That is when you have to dig down and remember that you ARE funny.

## The scientist

Dr Selina Wray is a senior research associate at UCL Institute of Neurology. She is pioneering development in the treatment of dementia.

## Selina's advice

I'm very lucky to work in a really diverse group — male, female, from all different backgrounds, all different nationalities — which is one of the things that I love about my job: getting to interact with people from across many different cultures . . . just all really enthusiastic about the science. My boss and head of department really believe that it doesn't matter where you come from in terms of background, ethnicity or anything — if you've got a passion for the science and you enjoy doing the science, you're welcome.

## The footballer

Girls kick ass at football. It is a brilliant career choice, and not just something you see when the Olympics is on TV. I spoke to Danielle Carter, who is twenty-three and a professional footballer. Danielle's proudest moment is scoring a hat-trick on her Senior England debut in the Lionesses.

## Danielle's advice

Be prepared to sacrifice your time. There will be times where you won't be able to attend certain events with friends, for example, as you'll have to prioritize your preparation for games/training. Once you finally get your breakthrough, continue to work as hard as you did, if not harder, to make sure you are the best you can be. And don't fall short or become complacent and get left behind!

Finally . . . ENJOY! Enjoy what you do and embrace your journey. Everyone's path in life is different; don't compare yours to anyone else . . . Be patient, work hard and keep the faith.

# TREADING ON YOUR OWN PATH

We've talked about the possibilities for your professional path and the importance of following your gut, your passion and thinking 'outside the box'. Life is not a neat form with little tick boxes that you check off. It doesn't work like that.

My advice? Spend time on yourself, get some experiences under your belt, challenge yourself with new things, explore your potential as far as you can and don't let what your peers are doing, or a newspaper headline, throw you off course. Chances are that once you are happy and secure in yourself and what you are doing, the other stuff will fall into place. But the most important thing to remember is that you don't have to have what everyone else has, or even want it, to be a valuable human being. You are amazing – just the way you are.

Me? I have had the dream job and realize that the dream always changes and I will never tire of new challenges. I got an A in my English GCSE and an E in Maths, and I didn't go to university. I am yet to have children and have no idea what will happen when I choose to do that. I have never been married. But, above all, I love deeply. That is the single most important thing to remember on your path. TO LOVE.

NOW GO REACH FOR THE MOOON!

# A LETTER TO MYSELF AGED 14

Dear Me

You don't have to rush. There is plenty of time to feel all the feelings there are to be felt. You will feel them all and, when you do, they will be huge. Though they will never stop being confusing, there is no light-bulb moment when it'll all make sense, no age between now and thirty-one where you will understand everything life throws at you. Your feelings will always change, just like your hair will. I know you think about these things every night before you go to sleep, but there is so much time for dancing, sparkly clothes, kissing and electric body tingles, so just wait a bit longer before you actually do them.

Keep letting the ridiculous ideas that flood your brain flow about like a song storm inside you. They are part of who you are and they will never stop. Remember when you were nine and you circled all the publishers in the 'P' section of the yellow pages, because you were gonna contact them to publish your book? You will write it one day.

Your boobs will get bigger too. So stop trying to think of ways you can make them bigger; stop researching those lie-herbal pills that promise to 'naturally enhance your bust' – it's a load of shit. A TOTAL load of shit. They will not enhance any bust. You will cringe so hard at the fact that you used to cross the straps of your padded bra at the back, squeezing your AA cups together to create the strangest-looking tiny cleavage. Quit whilst you're ahead. Oh, and you don't need to wear foundation, honestly you don't. Your skin is amazing, even with those spots on your forehead. The limited choice of foundation shades you can get in your town are completely wrong for you and, if I'm honest, make your face look like it's been smeared in a light dusting of chalk. By the way, the spots will disappear and the scars don't even stay, so stop hating your face.

The rest of you will get bigger too, but never focus too hard on how much. Your body will change with the times, as will your brain. It will adapt to the world around you, which'll be a fun one, I promise. Your body will be loved and treated with tender loving care by others, so try to learn to do the same. Exhaust yourself by playing and exploring, you don't need to think about exercise, just keep thrashing about. Drink loads of water, like at any given opportunity, guzzle, guzzle, gulp, glug it.

Never be ashamed of who you are. Sometimes you are, as they say, 'a bit much', 'too loud' and 'quite annoying', but who gives a f*ck? Especially as the good people in your life will like you that way. You can live your own story and it doesn't have to be anybody else's. Listen to your gut, it makes even better decisions than your brain or your heart does sometimes.

You don't have to be like anyone else: no celebrity, prefect at your school or anyone else you've come across or know. Listen to your weirdness – it comes from having a gigantic imagination and boundless hope. It will always help you to appreciate colour, travel, nature and many types of people. There are extraordinary people everywhere on this planet, so even when you think the world is too awful to bear, trust in your love of exploring, talking, dancing and staring at vast open spaces and the twinkling sea – it'll see you through and keep your perspective fresh. Be proud of your ability to love your friends, but beware of the toxic ones.

Keep loving new opportunities and new ways of experiencing things. You don't have a 'bad attitude', like some of the teachers say you do. Try to learn to channel the energy and the incessant question-asking into learning rather than bedazzling mischief. You will always love to be mischievous, but will learn that the best way is to mix it with good – it's still *well* fun, but feels better peppered with a little sophistication and creativity. Being plain bad is boring and guilt-ridden.

Keep reading, keep writing. Keep asking the big, hard questions about things that don't feel right in life, things that are unjust. But you don't have to scream them, even if the truth makes you rage and your face hot. You don't always know what's right, no one single person does. You have more power than you think. Engage in politics and keep absorbing history with the inquisitive, spongy nature you have. You are far from stupid even though you will always be catastrophic at maths. You will never know what you want to be when you grow up, and will realize that most people don't.

You're going to be all right. There isn't as much struggle as you subconsciously prepare for.

Ask for help, rather than getting angry. Anger rusts a person's morals and clouds vision, it doesn't suit you, so breathe deep – you will learn to be happy and you are not a bad person. Bad is a bad word to apply to yourself unless you are dancing to a Michael Jackson song or using the term 'badass'.

You don't have to give in emotionally to a love that feels out of control. You are strong and you have more control than you think. You have time to run to where it is safer. You *can* get out of this. If the love feels bad and unhealthy, if it makes you mostly sad, it isn't a good love. There are others out there, willing to give you a good love, so break up with the boy who is hurting you. Honestly, I know you can't imagine it, but get out of it now. It'll be so much better for you in the end if you do.

Keep your mind open. Don't judge others or abide by the constraints of the imposed class system or stereotyping. Don't forget, no one is too special or not good enough to communicate with. You will learn something from nearly everyone you meet.

Please stop shaving your bikini line, the shaving-rash marks will remain forever.

Be you and keep your head held high.

Love Gem
Aged 31

# USEFUL WEBSITES

## YOUR MIND
www.sane.org.uk
www.mind.org.uk

### Counselling/Psychotherapy
www.icap.org.uk
www.bacp.co.uk
www.counsellingfoundation.org

### Depression
www.mind.org.uk/information-support/types-
of-mental-health-problems/depression
www.pandasfoundation.org.uk
www.rethink.org/diagnosis-treatment/
conditions/depression

### Suicide Charities
www.samaritans.org.uk
www.allianceofhope.org
www.maytree.org.uk

### Eating Disorders
www.anorexiabulimiacare.org.uk
www.b-eat.co.uk
www.seedeatingdisorders.org.uk

### OCD
www.ocduk.org
www.ocdaction.org.uk

### Addiction
www.actiononaddiction.org.uk
www.addaction.org.uk
www.lighthousefoundation.org.uk

### Self-Harm
www.selfharm.co.uk
www.selfinjurysupport.org.uk

## YOUR WORLD AND YOUR FUTURE

### Politics
www.globalissues.org
www.theyworkforyou.com

### The Planet
www.greenpeace.org.uk
Mentoring & Volunteering
www.arts-emergency.org
www.megaphonewrite.com
www.womentoringproject.co.uk
www.princes-trust.org.uk
www.timebank.org.uk/

### The Internet
www.bbc.co.uk/webwise
www.revengepornhelpline.org.uk

### Online Magazines
www.gal-dem.com
www.thatswhatss.com

### Missing People
www.missingpeople.org.uk

# THANK YOU!

A thanks and a big-up to Paradise Apartments and Alex's Bar in Sarakiniko, for putting up with me meandering around the gaff like a crazed pup with computers for eyes and leaving me to it, typing like a nut in apartment No. 9. A time never to be forgotten, days before the EU Referendum vote; the internet turning me sometimes into a sobbing mess.

Thank you, Mrs Dragon, for your perfect combination of warm and smiley wicked giggles. Plus little Riko too, for merely providing the brilliance and innocence of a baby genius who loves the sea even more than I do.

Thank you to Sara Jane at the Coach House, for providing the perfect solitary escape.

Thank you, Jim, I love you – I have been a NIGHTMARE. 2016: nightmare girlfriend – you survived it!

Thank you, Becky Thomas, for listening to my hare-brained idea, when I collared you in a stinky pub. Thank you, Emily, for being my carer. Thank you, Rachel P and Gaby, for reining me in. Thank you, Rachel V, for not writing swear words back when I was being so clueless and yet bossy in my emails. Thank you, Kat, for sharing the wheels-on-the-bus-going-round-and-round vision from the get-go. Thank you to Bea, for your lovely energy of enthusiasm and care for this project! Thank you to all of team *Open*. YOU are AMAZING.

Thank you, Aurelia. WOW you have blown us away. Anyone who takes a manic message about a smiling condom and makes it into an iconic picture is frankly magnificent.

Thank you, SJ, for being the slickest and most resilient life cheerleader always.

Thank you, Woo, for ALWAYS feeding and challenging my brain, and for listening to me relentlessly wang ON.

Thank you, BriGaz, you are a treasure to know – and give endless inspiration and love.

Thank you to ALL ma crew. My friends for always nodding when I'm chatting tripe, scooping me up when I go crazy, never making me feel judged or misunderstood, for being the BEST FUN. YEP, that's you, brother from another mother and deep inspiration Laurence (aka Lozini); you, my forever bestie Camilla (CamCam); Scott (Scottie-too-hottie); beautiful and kind Sarah (Baker), Sam (aka monsieur le mayor) and your new addition baby Bow; Dallanda (aka Trojan), gorgeous Niklas and your magic Baby Issaga; determined and brilliant Claudia (Cloudini) and Matt (Clark Kent), thank you for always supporting me in the *Birmingham Mail*. Thank you, Amy (Zing), for being as warm and colourful as a walking rainbow and introducing me to a home town I could find the calm to write a book in.

Thank you to Katie V, for trawling through lots of gabbing.

Thanks, Amber and Rob, for not batting an eyelid when I was a sweaty monster furiously typing in my room and regurgitating angst during the process.

Thank you to the boyz, all of the loves of the past mentioned in *Open*, for you have taught me so much. It's cos of you I know how to love and how to heal.

Thank you to Becky and Daniella, the most patient and talented videographers in the country.

Thank you, Nash and Dockers, for being gifted, wordy dreamers and for making feel like I could be the same.

Thank you to all those at the Beeb, who trained me up good and proper, and believed in me to give the opportunities that you have.

Thank you to those in my industry who I count as dear and supportive friends and mad-core inspirationals – that's you, Lala & Dawn.

Thank you to Mum, Laura and Daddy Cool for continuously putting up with me.

AND OF COURSE ALL THE CONTRIBUTORSSSSS . . . You were too ace for me not to include you in this book.

AISLING BEA > PAGE 143
© KARLA GOWLETT

AURELIA LANGE >
ILLUSTRATOR

KAREN BLACKETT
OBE > PAGE 131

JOSIE LONG > PAGE 72

LITERARY AGENT >

JANENE SPENCER >
DESIGNER

RACHEL VALE >
ART DIRECTOR

FRANCES ACQUAAH >
PAGE 76

AN GLASER > AGES 5 + 42

DAME HEATHER RABBATTS > PAGE 132

ASHLEY FULWOOD > PAGE 33

LIV GAL-DEM > PAGE 102

LAURA DARRALL > PAGE 22

HANNA YUSUF > PAGE 114
© ELIAS YONIS

GEORGE LESTER > ASSISTANT EDITOR

DR ALISON ATTRILL-SMITH > PAGE 93

CAROLINE ROTHSTEIN > PAGE 30
© CHRISTOPHER CLAUSS

KAT MCKENNA > MARKETING MANAGER

LUCY > PAGE 120

DR CAROLINE TAYLOR > PAGE 14

EMILY THOMAS > EDITOR

MARAWA CAMARA > PAGE 140

JUNE ERIC-UDORIE > PAGE 130

EDITORIAL DIRECTOR NON-FICTION & POETRY > GABY MORGAN

DR SELINA WRAY > PAGE 144

ANONYMOUS SELF-HARMER > PAGE 48

JO SWINSON > PAGE 71

LEO PEMBERTON > PAGE 29

DANIELLE CARTER > PAGE 144

BEA CROSS > PUBLICITY MANAGER

KAREN ROBINSON > PAGE 110

IZZY > PAGE 104

BEEKEEPER BECCA > PAGE 82

RACHEL PETTY > EDITORIAL DIRECTOR

KATIE V > TRANSCRIBING WHIZZ

SUSIE ORBACH > PAGE 28

# INDEX